S0-AZU-367

SCOTT FORESMAN · ADDISON WESLEY

Mathematics

Grade 1

Reteaching
Masters/
Workbook

PEARSON

Scott
Foresman

Editorial Offices: Glenview, Illinois • Parsippany, New Jersey • New York, New York

Sales Offices: Needham, Massachusetts • Duluth, Georgia • Glenview, Illinois
Coppell, Texas • Ontario, California • Mesa, Arizona

Overview

Reteaching Masters/Workbook provides additional teaching options for teachers to use with students who have not yet mastered key skills and concepts covered in the student edition. A pictorial model is provided when appropriate, followed by worked-out examples and a few partially worked-out exercises. These exercises match or are similar to the simpler exercises in the student edition.

ISBN 0-328-11683-1

Copyright © Pearson Education, Inc.

All Rights Reserved. Printed in the United States of America. This publication, or parts thereof, may be used with appropriate equipment to reproduce copies for classroom use only.

4 5 6 7 8 9 10 V084 09 08 07 06 05

Making 6

We can show 6 in different ways.

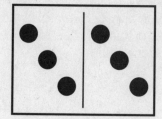 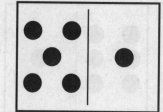

___3___ and ___3___   ___5___ and ___1___

Write the numbers that show ways to make 6.

1.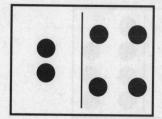

___2___ and ___4___

2.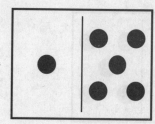

_____ and _____

3.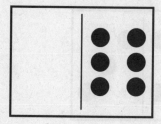

_____ and _____

4.

_____ and _____

© Pearson Education, Inc. 1

Name _____

Making 7

We can show 7 in different ways.

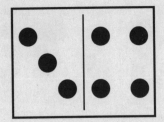   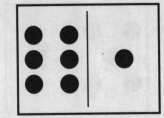

__3__ and __4__   __6__ and __1__

Write the numbers that show ways to make 7.

1.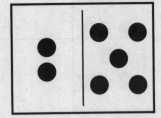

__2__ and __5__

2.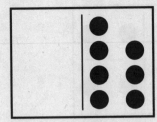

_____ and _____

3.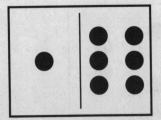

_____ and _____

4.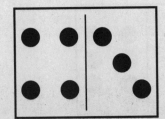

_____ and _____

© Pearson Education, Inc. 1

Making 8 and 9

We can make 9 in different ways.

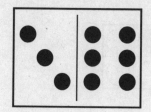 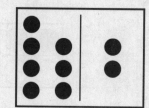 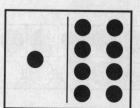

__3__ and __6__   __7__ and __2__   __1__ and __8__

Write the numbers that show ways to make 8 and 9.

1.

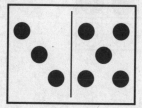

__3__ and __5__

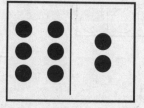

_____ and _____

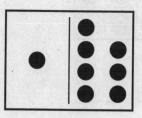

_____ and _____

2.

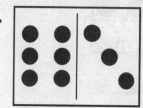

_____ and _____

_____ and _____

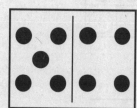

_____ and _____

© Pearson Education, Inc. 1

Making 10

Here are some different ways to make 10.

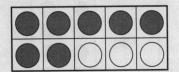

7 and 3

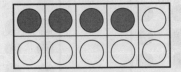

4 and 6

Write the numbers that show ways to make 10.

1.

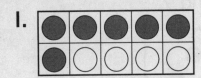

__6__ and __4__

2.

_____ and _____

3.

_____ and _____

4.

_____ and _____

5.

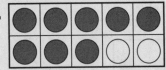

_____ and _____

6.

_____ and _____

© Pearson Education, Inc. 1

Name _____

Use Objects

What different ways can you put
9 counters on Workmat 1?

Workmat 1

┌─────────────┐
│   1   │
└─────────────┘

(**Read and Understand**)

There are 9 counters in all.

(**Plan and Solve**)

Put 2 counters on the left part
and 7 counters on the right part.
Move 1 counter from the
right side to the left side.
Write the numbers.

(**Look Back and Check**)

How do you know your answer
is correct?

In All

2	7	9
3		9
		9

Pat wants to put all 9 dots on the clown hats.
She wants to put some dots on each hat.
Use counters for dots and
paper for hats. What other ways
can you put 9 dots on 2 clown hats?
Write the numbers.

1. __2__ and __7__

2. ____ and ____

© Pearson Education, Inc. 1

Name _____

1 and 2 More Than

We can find one more than a number.

Count.
There are 4.

Count.
There are 5.

4 and 1 more
4 and 1 more is 5.

We can find two more than a number.

Count.
There are 4.

Count.
There are 6.

4 and 2 more
4 and 2 more is 6.

Use counters to show one and two more.
Write the numbers.

1.

5 and 1 more is __6__.

5 and 2 more is _____.

2.

9 and 1 more is _____.

9 and 2 more is _____.

3.

6 and 2 more is _____.

6 and 1 more is _____.

© Pearson Education, Inc. 1

Name _____

1 and 2 Fewer Than

We can find one fewer than a number.

Show 6.	Cross out 1.	Now there are 5.

I fewer than 6 is 5.

We can find two fewer than a number.

Show 4.	Cross out 2.	Now there are 2.

2 fewer than 4 is 2.

Use counters to show one and two fewer.
Cross out counters. Write the numbers.

1.

   I fewer than 7 is __6__.

2.

   2 fewer than 8 is _____.

Problem Solving *Algebra*

Use counters to show one and two fewer.
Write the numbers.

3.

   I fewer than _____ is 8.

4.

   2 fewer than _____ is 7.

© Pearson Education, Inc. 1

Comparing Numbers to 5 and to 10

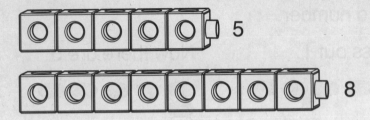 5

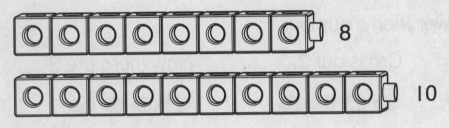 8

8 is more than 5.

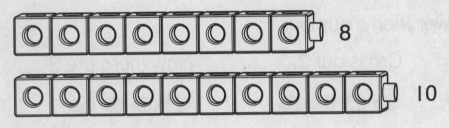 8

 10

8 is fewer than 10.

Use cubes. Circle **more** or **fewer**.

1. 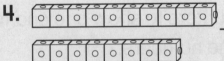 10
7

more   fewer

10 is _____ than 7.

2. _____

more   fewer

5 is _____ than 7.

3. _____

more   fewer

5 is _____ than 3.

4. _____

more   fewer

10 is _____ than 8.

© Pearson Education, Inc. 1

Ordering Numbers Through 12

We can put numbers in order.

 2 is the least.

 4

> The numbers are in order from least to greatest.

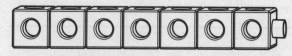 7 is the greatest.

Use cubes. Write the numbers in order from least to greatest.

1. 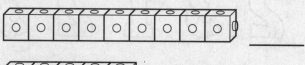 5   3 is the least.

3   8 is the greatest.

8

2. _____   _____ is the least.

_____   _____ is the greatest.

_____

3. _____   _____ is the least.

_____   _____ is the greatest.

_____

© Pearson Education, Inc. 1

Identifying the Pattern Unit

This is a pattern.

  repeats over and over.

This is a pattern, too.

repeats over and over.

Circle the pattern unit.

I.

2.

3.

© Pearson Education, Inc. 1

Translating Patterns

Look at these patterns.

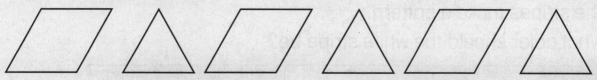

| A | B | A | B | A | B |

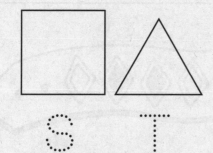 repeats over and over. AB repeats over and over.

Use pattern blocks. Make a pattern. Draw the pattern.
Then make the same pattern using letters.

I.

A   B   A   B   A   B

2.

S   T

© Pearson Education, Inc. 1

PROBLEM-SOLVING SKILL
Use Data from a Picture

The stripes make a pattern.

What color should the white stripe be?

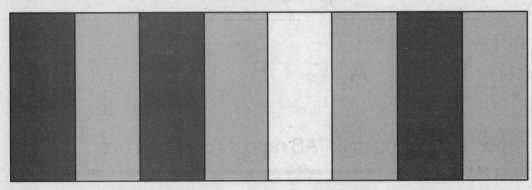

Find the pattern.

Color what is missing.

1.

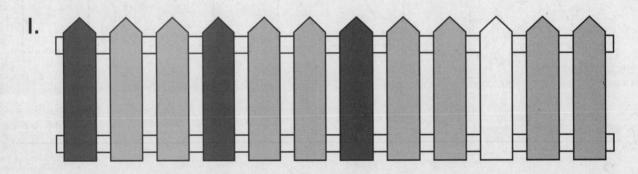

2.

© Pearson Education, Inc. 1

Name _____

It's a Party!

This is a pattern. The balloon and party hat repeat
over and over.

Find the pattern. Draw what comes next.

1.    _____

2.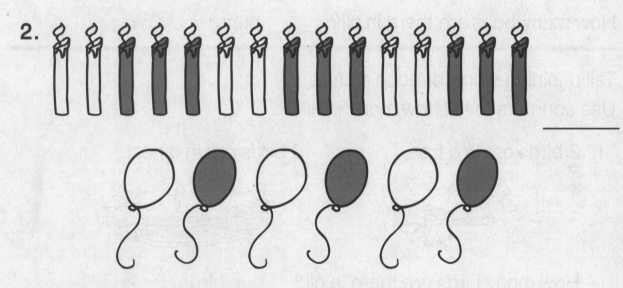

                                                                _____

3. How many white balloons are there? _____

4. How many gray balloons are there? _____

5. What color should come next in the pattern? _____

6. If Jeff wants 11 balloons, how many more
   balloons does he need?

   _____ more balloons

© Pearson Education, Inc. 1

Stories About Joining

Join the groups to find how many bugs
there are in all.

Place a counter on each bug. Then count.

2 bugs are on the rock.

3 bugs are on the blanket.

1   2   3   4   5

How many bugs are there in all? _____ bugs

Tell a joining story for each picture.
Use counters to tell how many in all.

1. 2 birds are in a tree.   2 birds are in a nest.

How many birds are there in all? _____ birds

2. 3 fish are in a bowl.   2 fish are in another bowl.

How many fish are there in all? _____ fish

© Pearson Education, Inc. 1

Using Counters to Add

Join the parts to make the whole.

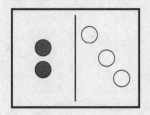

How many black counters? __2__

How many white counters? __3__

__2__ and __3__ is __5__ in all. 5 is the sum of 2 and 3.

Add to find the sum. Use counters if you like.

I.

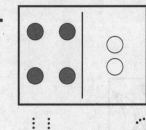

How many black counters?

How many white counters?

__4__ and __2__ is __6__ in all. 6 is the sum of 4 and 2.

2.

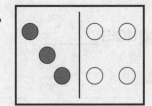

_____ and _____ is _____ in all.

3.

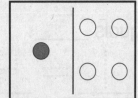

_____ and _____ is _____ in all.

4.

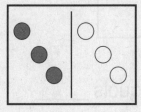

_____ and _____ is _____ in all.

5.

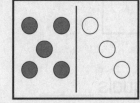

_____ and _____ is _____ in all.

© Pearson Education, Inc. 1

Using Numbers to Add

Find how many in all.

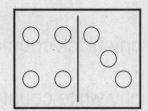

    __4__ and   __3__   is   __7__ in all.

    __4__ plus   __3__ equals __7__.

    4   +   3   =   7

> This is an addition sentence.

Tell how many in all.

Then write an addition sentence.

1.

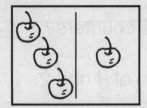

3 plus 1 equals __4__.

__3__ + __1__ = __4__

2.

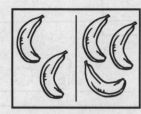

2 plus 3 equals ____.

____ + ____ = ____

3.

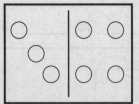

3 plus 4 equals ____.

____ + ____ = ____

4.

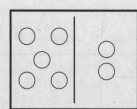

5 plus 2 equals ____.

____ + ____ = ____

© Pearson Education, Inc. 1

Zero in Addition

How many in each part? How many in all?

$$3 + 0 = 3$$

$$0 + 4 = 4$$

Write an addition sentence.

1.

$$2 + 0 = 2$$

2.

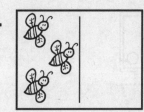

$$\_\_ + 0 = \_\_$$

3.

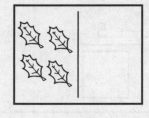

$$\_\_ + \_\_ = \_\_$$

4.

$$\_\_ + \_\_ = \_\_$$

5.

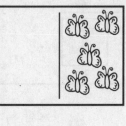

$$\_\_ + \_\_ = \_\_$$

6.

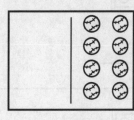

$$\_\_ + \_\_ = \_\_$$

© Pearson Education, Inc. 1

Vertical Addition

There are two ways to show addition.

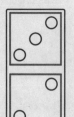

$$\begin{array}{r} 3 \\ +\ 2 \\ \hline 5 \end{array}$$

The sum is the same both ways.

3 + 2 = 5

Add to find the sum.

1.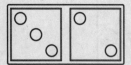

4 + 3 = __7__

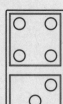

$$\begin{array}{r} 4 \\ +\ 3 \\ \hline 7 \end{array}$$

2.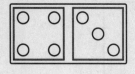

2 + 5 = ____

$$\begin{array}{r} 2 \\ +\ 5 \\ \hline \square \end{array}$$

3.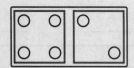

4 + 2 = ____

$$\begin{array}{r} 4 \\ +\ 2 \\ \hline \square \end{array}$$

4.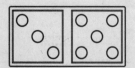

3 + 5 = ____

$$\begin{array}{r} 3 \\ +\ 5 \\ \hline \square \end{array}$$

© Pearson Education, Inc. 1

Write a Number Sentence

Write an addition sentence to solve a problem.

2 dogs are sitting.

3 dogs are standing.

How many dogs are there in all?

Read and Understand

You need to find how many dogs there are in all.

Plan and Solve

You can write an addition sentence.

$$2 + 3 = 5$$

Look Back and Check

Does your answer make sense?

Write an addition sentence to answer the question.

1. You have 4 books.
   You get 1 more book.
   How many books do
   you have in all?

   _____ + _____ = _____

2. There are 3 frogs.
   4 more frogs come.
   How many frogs are
   there in all?

   _____ + _____ = _____

© Pearson Education, Inc. 1

Stories About Separating

Count to find how many are left.
Use counters to help you.

Jeff has 5 balloons.
2 balloons fly away.
How many balloons
does he have left?

 balloons

Use counters to answer each question.

1. There are 6 cars.
   2 cars drive away.
   How many cars
   are left?

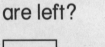 cars

2. There are 7 cats.
   3 are sleeping.
   The rest are playing.
   How many cats
   are playing?

 cats

© Pearson Education, Inc. 1

Name _____

Using Counters to Subtract

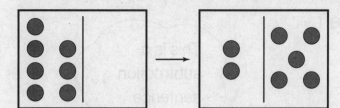

How many counters do we begin with? __7__

How many counters do we take away? __2__

How many are left? __5__

7 take away 2 leaves __5__.

Subtract to find the difference.
Use counters if you like.

1.

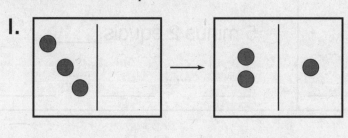

_____ take away _____ leaves _____.

2.

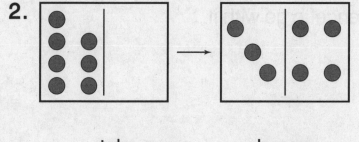

_____ take away _____ leaves _____.

© Pearson Education, Inc. 1

Use with Lesson 2-8. **21**

Using Numbers to Subtract

Subtract to find how many are left.

<table>
<tr><td>___5___</td><td>take away</td><td>___2___</td><td>is</td><td>___3___.</td></tr>
<tr><td>___5___</td><td>minus</td><td>___2___</td><td>equals</td><td>___3___.</td></tr>
<tr><td>5</td><td>−</td><td>2</td><td>=</td><td>3</td></tr>
</table>

This is a subtraction sentence.

Write a subtraction sentence.

1.

4 minus 1 equals __3__.

4 — 1 = 3

2.

5 minus 2 equals _____.

___ ___ ___ ___ ___

Problem Solving *Writing in Math*

3. Draw a picture that shows subtraction.
Write a subtraction sentence to go with it.

© Pearson Education, Inc. 1

Zero in Subtraction

> If you take away all, zero are left.

> If you take away zero, all are left.

$$5 - 5 = 0 \qquad 5 - 0 = 5$$

Write a subtraction sentence.

1.

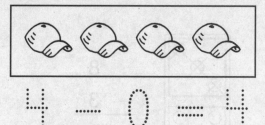

$$4 - 0 = 4$$

2.

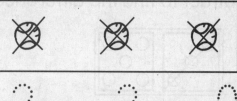

$$3 - 3 = 0$$

3.

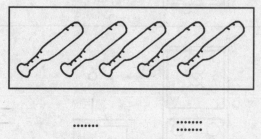

_____ .... _____ .... _____

4.

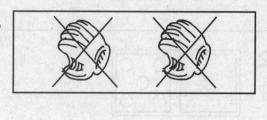

_____ .... _____ .... _____

5.

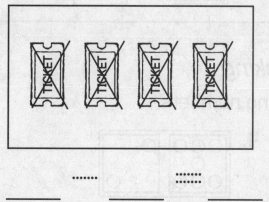

_____ .... _____ .... _____

6.

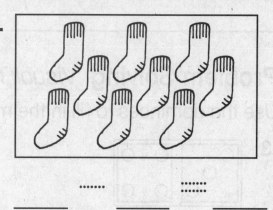

_____ .... _____ .... _____

© Pearson Education, Inc. 1

Vertical Subtraction

There are two ways to show subtraction.

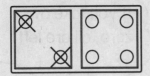

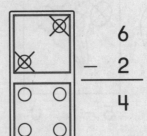

$$\begin{array}{r} 6 \\ -\ 2 \\ \hline 4 \end{array}$$

> The answer is the same both ways.

$6 - 2 = 4$

Subtract to find the difference.

1.

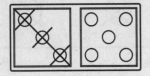

$$\begin{array}{r} 8 \\ -\ 3 \\ \hline 5 \end{array}$$

$8 - 3 = \underline{5}$

2.

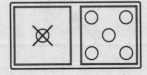

$$\begin{array}{r} 6 \\ -\ 1 \\ \hline \square \end{array}$$

$6 - 1 = \underline{}$

Problem Solving *Visual Thinking*

Use the dominoes to fill in the missing numbers.

3.

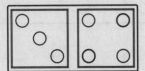

$7 - \underline{} = 4$

4.

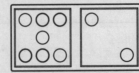

$\underline{} - 7 = 2$

© Pearson Education, Inc. 1

PROBLEM-SOLVING SKILL

Choose an Operation

Take away 2 flowers.

How many are left?

add   subtract

_3_ flowers

Use the picture. Choose **add** or **subtract**.

Write the answer.

---

1. 6 watermelons are in the garden.
   2 are in the basket.
   How many watermelons are there in all?

   add   subtract

   _____ watermelons

---

2. There are 9 carrots.
   2 are picked.
   How many carrots are left
   in the garden?

   add   subtract

   _____ carrots

---

3. 5 tomato plants are in one row.
   6 corn plants are in the same row.
   How many plants in all are in the row?

   add   subtract

   _____ plants

© Pearson Education, Inc. 1

Using Cubes to Compare

Match the white cubes with the gray cubes.
Then count how many more.

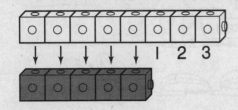

How many more
white cubes? ____3____ more white cubes

How many fewer
gray cubes? ____3____ fewer gray cubes

Write how many white cubes and how many gray cubes.
Then write how many more and how many fewer.

1.
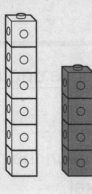

__4__ white cubes

__2__ gray cubes

__2__ more white
cubes

2.

____ white cubes

____ gray cubes

____ more white
cubes

3.
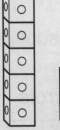

____ white cubes

____ gray cubes

____ fewer gray
cubes

4.
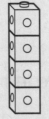
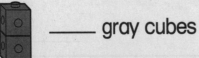

____ white cubes

____ gray cubes

____ fewer gray
cube

© Pearson Education, Inc. 1

Using Subtraction to Compare

Write a subtraction sentence to compare.

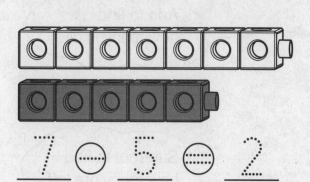

There are __2__ more white cubes than gray cubes.

There are __2__ fewer gray cubes than white cubes.

Write a subtraction sentence.

1. How many more socks than shoes?

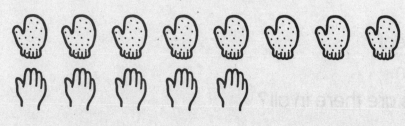

_____ ◯ _____ ◯ _____   _____ more socks

2. How many fewer hands than mittens?

_____ ◯ _____ ◯ _____   _____ fewer hands

© Pearson Education, Inc. 1

Name _____

Bugs, Bugs, Everywhere!

There are 4 ants.

2 more ants join them.

How many ants are
there in all?

> Add to find
> how many in all.

$$4 + 2 = 6$$

There are 6 ants.

4 ants leave.

How many ants
are left?

> Subtract to find
> how many are left.

$$6 - 4 = 2$$

Circle the correct number sentence.

Write the answer.

1. There are 5 bees on a flower.

   3 bees fly away.

   How many bees are left?

   $5 + 3 = 8$ $5 - 3 = 2$ There are _____ bees left.

2. 7 bugs sit on a leaf.

   2 bugs join them.

   How many bugs are there in all?

   $7 + 2 = 9$ $7 - 2 = 5$ There are _____ bugs in all.

© Pearson Education, Inc. 1

Counting On 1, 2, or 3

There are 5 cubes in the box.	Add 2 more cubes.		Start with 5.	Count on 2 more.

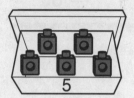

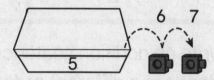

$$5 \; + \; 2 \; = \; \underline{7}$$

1.

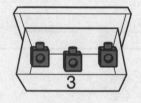

Start with ___3___.   Count on ___1___ more.

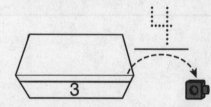

$$3 + 1 = \underline{4}$$

Count on to find the sum.
Use cubes if you like.

2.

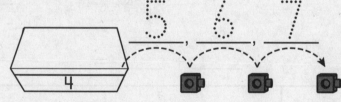

$$4 + 3 = \underline{}$$

3.

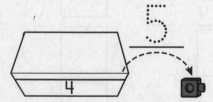

$$4 + 1 = \underline{}$$

© Pearson Education, Inc. 1

Adding in Any Order

You can add in any order and get the same sum.

$$4 + 2 = 6$$

$$2 + 4 = 6$$

Add. Write an addition sentence with
the addends in a different order.

1.

<u>5</u> + <u>2</u> = <u>7</u>   <u>2</u> + <u>5</u> = <u>7</u>

2.

<u>4</u> + <u>1</u> = ____   ____ + ____ = ____

3.

____ + ____ = ____   ____ + ____ = ____

---

4. 5
   + 4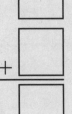

5. 3
   + 4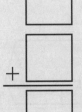

© Pearson Education, Inc. 1

Name _____

Adding 1, 2, or 3

You start with the greater number when you count on.

◯◯◯◯◯   ◯ ◯

　　5　　　　+　　2　　= ____

5 is the greater number. Count on.

◯◯◯◯◯  ⑥ ⑦

　　5　　　　+　　2　　= 7

Circle the greater number. Then count on to add.

1.

(5)　+　1　=　6

2.

◯　◯◯◯
◯　◯◯◯

　2　+　(6)　= ____

3.

◯◯　◯
◯◯　◯◯
　5　+　3　= ____

4.

　　◯◯
◯◯　◯◯
◯
　3　+　4　= ____

5. 5 + 6 = ____

6. 7 + 4 = ____

7. 1 + 10 = ____

8. 9 + 3 = ____

9. 2 + 8 = ____

10. 7 + 1 = ____

© Pearson Education, Inc. 1

Adding Using a Number Line

To help you count on, circle the number you start at.
Draw to show the addition on the number line.

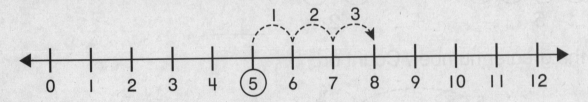

$$5 + 3 = \underline{8}$$

Add 1, 2, or 3. Use the number line to help you.

1. $4 + 3 = \underline{7}$

2. $2 + 6 = \underline{}$

3. $3 + 6 = \underline{}$

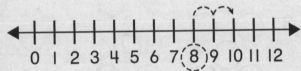

4. $8 + 2 = \underline{}$

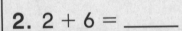

5.
$$\begin{array}{r} 9 \\ + 3 \\ \hline \end{array}$$

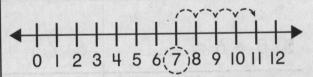

6.
$$\begin{array}{r} 7 \\ + 4 \\ \hline \end{array}$$

© Pearson Education, Inc. 1

Name _____

PROBLEM-SOLVING SKILL
Extra Information

Cross out the information you do not need.
Solve the problem.

> You can underline the sentence that tells what you need to find out.

Dan has 2 dogs.
~~He has one bike.~~
He has 3 cats.
How many pets does Dan have in all?

$\underline{2} + \underline{3} = \underline{5}$ pets

Cross out the information you do not need.
Then write a number sentence to solve the problem.

1. Lin read 3 books last month.
   She read 4 books this month.
   2 of the books were about horses.
   How many books did Lin read in all?

   $\underline{3} + \underline{4} = \underline{7}$ books

---

2. Tom has 6 model cars. He has 1 model train.
   Tom gets 2 more model cars.
   How many model cars does Tom have altogether?

   _____ + _____ = _____ model cars

---

3. 1 frog jumps in the water. 2 ducks fly away.
   Then 4 more ducks fly away.
   How many ducks fly away in all?

   _____ + _____ = _____ ducks

© Pearson Education, Inc. 1

Doubles

You can use a double to add.

Both addends are the same. They are doubles.

$$2 + 2 = 4 \qquad 3 + 3 = 6$$

Write an addition sentence for each double.

1.

$$4 + 4 = 8$$

2.

$$6 + \underline{} = \underline{}$$

3.

$$\underline{} + \underline{} = \underline{}$$

4.

$$\underline{} + \underline{} = \underline{}$$

5.

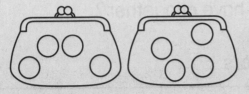

How many coins are there in all?

$$\underline{} + \underline{} = \underline{}$$

6.

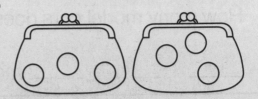

How many coins are there in all?

$$\underline{} + \underline{} = \underline{}$$

© Pearson Education, Inc. 1

Doubles Plus I

We can use doubles to add other numbers.

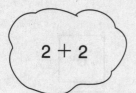   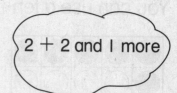

$$2 + 2 = 4 \qquad 2 + 3 = 5$$

Find each sum. Use counters if you like.

1.

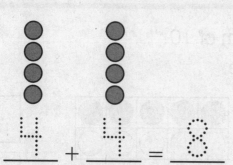

$$\underline{} + \underline{} = \underline{8} \qquad\qquad \underline{} + \underline{5} = \underline{}$$

2.

$$\underline{} + \underline{} = \underline{} \qquad\qquad \underline{} + \underline{} = \underline{}$$

Write a double or a double plus one for each sum.

3.

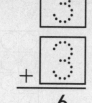

3	3		4		
+ 3	+	+ 4	+	+	+
6	7	8	9	10	11

© Pearson Education, Inc. 1

Sums of 10

Each ten-frame stands for a group of 10.
You can use a ten-frame to learn sums of 10.

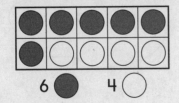

6 ● 4 ○

$6 + 4 = 10$

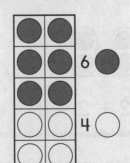

Fill in the missing numbers to find a sum of 10.
Use ten-frames and counters if you like.

1.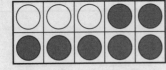

$\underline{3} + \underline{7} = 10$

$\begin{array}{r} 3 \\ + 7 \\ \hline 10 \end{array}$

2.

$\underline{} + \underline{5} = 10$

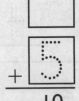
$\begin{array}{r} \\ + 5 \\ \hline 10 \end{array}$

3.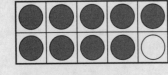

$\underline{} + \underline{} = 10$

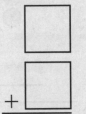
$\begin{array}{r} \\ + \\ \hline 10 \end{array}$

4.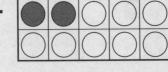

$\underline{} + \underline{} = 10$

$\begin{array}{r} \\ + \\ \hline 10 \end{array}$

---

5. Circle the ten-frame that shows your answer.

Ben has 8 gray counters.
How many white counters does
he need to have 10 counters?

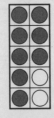  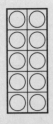

© Pearson Education, Inc. 1

Name _____

There are 4 blue buttons.
There are 3 red buttons.
How many buttons are there?

Blue Buttons	Red Buttons

Read and Understand

You need to find how many buttons
there are in all.

Plan and Solve

You can draw a picture of the buttons.
Then you can write a number sentence.
Count the buttons in your picture to find the sum.

$$4 + 3 = 7$$

$4 + 3 = 7$ buttons

Look Back and Check

How can you be sure your answer is correct?

Draw a picture.
Then write a number sentence.

Bird Stamps   **Cat Stamps**

1. Dan has 2 bird stamps.
   He gets 4 cat stamps.
   How many stamps are there altogether?

   _____ stamps   _____ + _____ = _____

© Pearson Education, Inc. 1

PROBLEM-SOLVING APPLICATIONS

Hop to It!

You can count on to add.

4 rabbits are in the house. 2 more rabbits come.
How many rabbits are there in all?

Start at 4.
Count on 5, 6.
$4 + 2 = 6$.

I.

5

$5 + 1 = 6$

2.

3

$3 + 3 = \underline{\quad}$

3.

6

$6 + 2 = \underline{\quad}$

---

4. There are 10 rabbits.
2 of them are in the house.
How many rabbits are outside? $2 + \underline{\quad} = 10$

---

5. There are 10 rabbits. 4 of them are outside.
How many rabbits are inside the house? $4 + \underline{\quad} = 10$

© Pearson Education, Inc. 1

Counting Back Using a Number Line

To find 7 − 2,
start at 7. Circle 7.

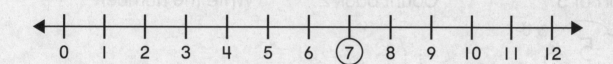

0 1 2 3 4 5 6 ⑦ 8 9 10 11 12

Now count back 2.

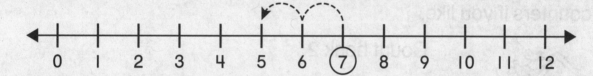

0 1 2 3 4 5 6 ⑦ 8 9 10 11 12

$7 - 2 = \underline{5}$

Count back to subtract.

Show your work on the number line.

1.

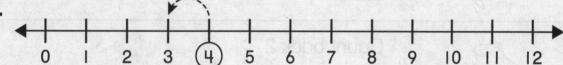

0 1 2 3 ④ 5 6 7 8 9 10 11 12

$4 - 1 = \underline{3}$

2.

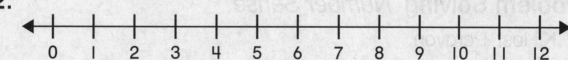

0 1 2 3 4 5 6 7 8 9 10 11 12

$9 - 2 = \underline{\hspace{2cm}}$

© Pearson Education, Inc. 1

Counting Back

You can count back to subtract 1 or 2.

$5 - 2 =$ _____

Start at 5.   Count back 2.   Write the number.

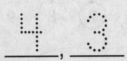

4, 3

$5 - 2 = 3$

Count back to subtract.
Use counters if you like.

1.    Count back 2.

3, _____

$4 - 2 =$ _____

2.    Count back 1.

_____

$8 - 1 =$ _____

3.    Count back 2.

_____, _____

$10 - 2 =$ _____

Problem Solving *Number Sense*

4. Kit lost 1 crayon.
   She only has 9 crayons now.
   How many crayons did she start with? _____

© Pearson Education, Inc. 1

Name _____

Using Doubles to Subtract

Doubles help you to subtract.

Think: $3 + 3 = \underline{6}$ so $6 - 3 = \underline{3}$

Add the doubles.
Then use the doubles to help you subtract.

1. $1 + 1 = \underline{2}$ so $2 - 1 = \underline{}$

2. $4 + 4 = \underline{}$ so $8 - 4 = \underline{}$

Problem Solving *Visual Thinking*

Complete the addition and subtraction sentences.

3. $2 + 2 = \underline{}$

    $4 - 2 = \underline{}$

© Pearson Education, Inc. 1

PROBLEM-SOLVING STRATEGY   **R 4-4**

Write a Number Sentence

There are 6 birds on the branch.
4 birds fly away.
How many birds are left?

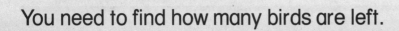

> **Read and Understand**

You need to find how many birds are left.

> **Plan and Solve**

Write a subtraction sentence to find how many birds are left.

$$6 - 4 = 2$$
___ ___ ___

> **Look Back and Check**

Does your answer make sense?

Write a subtraction sentence to answer each question.

1. There are 8 marbles in the bag.
   3 marbles roll out.
   How many marbles
   are left in the bag?

   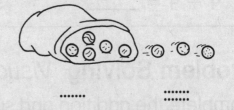

   _____ _____ _____

2. Mary has 10 pencils.
   She gives 4 pencils to Jack.
   How many pencils does
   Mary have left?

   _____ _____ _____

© Pearson Education, Inc. 1

Name _____

Using Related Facts

$4 + 3 = 7$

$7 - 3 = 4$

> The addition fact and the subtraction fact use the same numbers.

$6 + 4 = \underline{10}$

$\underline{10} - 4 = \underline{6}$

> The sum of the addition sentence is the first number in the subtraction sentence.

Write a related addition and subtraction sentence for each picture.

1.

$\underline{7} + \underline{4} = \underline{11}$

$\underline{11} - \underline{4} = \underline{7}$

2.

$\underline{} + \underline{2} = \underline{}$

$\underline{} - \underline{2} = \underline{}$

3.

$\underline{} + \underline{} = \underline{}$

$\underline{} - \underline{} = \underline{}$

4.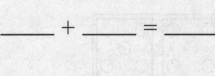

$\underline{} + \underline{} = \underline{}$

$\underline{} - \underline{} = \underline{}$

© Pearson Education, Inc. 1

Fact Families

This is a fact family.

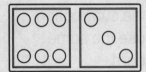

$6 + 3 = 9$ $9 - 3 = 6$

$3 + \underline{6} = 9$ $9 - \underline{6} = 3$

There are four related facts in this fact family.

This is a fact family, too.

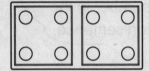

$4 + 4 = \underline{8}$ $8 - 4 = \underline{4}$

There are two related facts in this fact family.

Write each fact family.

1.
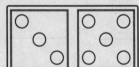

$\underline{3} + \underline{} = \underline{}$ $\underline{} - \underline{3} = \underline{}$

$\underline{} + \underline{3} = \underline{}$ $\underline{} - \underline{} = \underline{3}$

2.
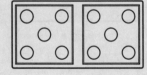

$\underline{} + \underline{} = \underline{}$ $\underline{} - \underline{} = \underline{}$

© Pearson Education, Inc. 1

Using Addition Facts to Subtract

Use addition facts to help you subtract.

6 − 1 = _____

5 + 1 = 6

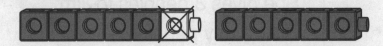

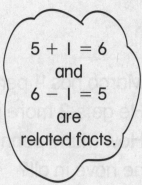

5 + 1 = 6
and
6 − 1 = 5
are
related facts.

6 − 1 = 5

Match the addition fact that will help you subtract. Then subtract.

1.

7 − 4 = 3

5 + 3 = 8

2.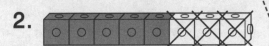

8 − 3 = _____

7 + 2 = 9

3.

6 − 4 = _____

2 + 4 = 6

4.

10 − 6 = _____

3 + 4 = 7

5.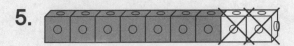

9 − 2 = _____

4 + 6 = 10

© Pearson Education, Inc. 1

Choose an Operation

Add to find how many in all.
Subtract to find how many are left.

Marco has 4 pennies. He gets 2 more pennies. How many pennies does he have in all?	Maria has 5 pennies. She gives 3 pennies to Jim. How many pennies does Maria have left?

(add)   subtract   add   (subtract)

$$4 \oplus 2 = 6 \qquad 5 \ominus 3 = 2$$

Circle add or subtract.

Then write a number sentence.

1. Ruth has 3 coins.
   She gives 1 coin to Bess.
   How many coins does Ruth have left?

   add   subtract

   _____ ◯ _____ = _____

2. Ned has 4 coins.
   He gets 3 more coins.
   How many coins does he have in all?

   add   subtract

   _____ ◯ _____ = _____

© Pearson Education, Inc. 1

Name _____

Playful Puppies

5 puppies play.

3 more puppies play.

How many puppies play in all?

__5__ + __3__ = __8__   __8__ puppies play

Solve. Use related facts to help you.

I. 8 puppies are sleeping and
   3 puppies wake up.
   How many puppies are still sleeping?

   _____ − _____ = _____   _____ puppies are sleeping

---

2. There are 8 puppies.
   There are 4 toys.
   Each puppy wants a toy.
   How many more toys are needed?

   _____ − _____ = _____   _____ more toys

---

3. There are 6 puppies.
   4 puppies go outside.
   How many puppies are still inside?

   _____ − _____ = _____   _____ puppies are inside

© Pearson Education, Inc. 1

Identifying Solid Figures

These shapes are solid figures.

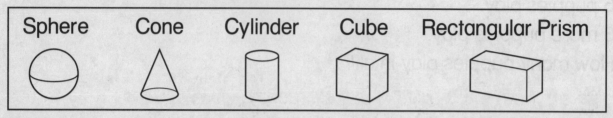

| Sphere | Cone | Cylinder | Cube | Rectangular Prism |

Color the spheres red. Color the cones blue.
Color the cylinders green. Color the cubes orange.
Color the rectangular prisms yellow.

I.

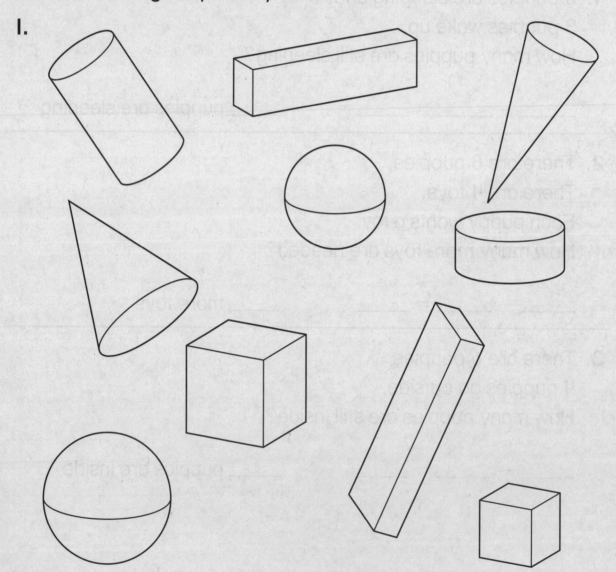

© Pearson Education, Inc. 1

Flat Surfaces and Vertices

These solid figures have flat surfaces.

 Cone   Cylinder

These solid figures have all flat surfaces called **faces**.

 Rectangular Prism   Cube

These solid figures have **vertices** or corners.

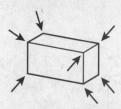   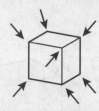

Use solid figures to complete the table.

Solid Figure	Number of Flat Surfaces	Number of Vertices (Corners)	Number of Faces
1. cube	6	8	6
2. cone			
3. rectangular prism			
4. cylinder			

© Pearson Education, Inc. 1

Name _____

Relating Plane Shapes to Solid Figures

R 5-3

If you trace around the flat surface, you can draw a
flat shape. Draw a line to the shape you would make.

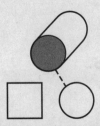 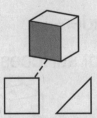 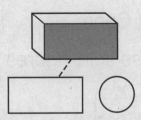

Look at the shape. Then circle the solid figure you
could trace to make the shape.

1.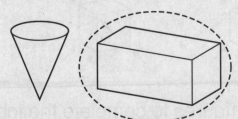

2.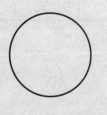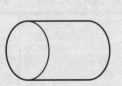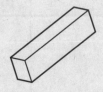

3.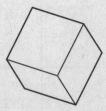

4.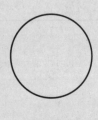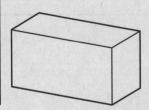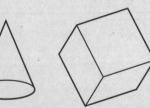

© Pearson Education, Inc. 1

50 Use with Lesson 5-3.

Identifying Plane Shapes

Plane Shapes

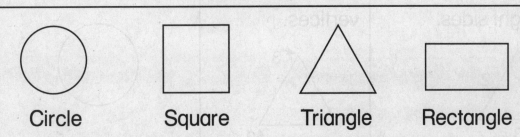

Circle   Square   Triangle   Rectangle

Color the shapes that are the same.

Circle the name.

1.

(square)

triangle

2.

square

circle

3.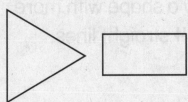

square

triangle

4.

rectangle

triangle

© Pearson Education, Inc. 1

Properties of Plane Shapes

Count the straight sides.	Count the vertices.	

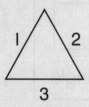

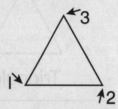

A triangle has _____ straight sides.

A triangle has _____ vertices.

A circle has _____ sides.

A circle has _____ vertices.

I.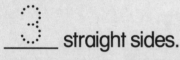

A square has _____ straight sides.

A square has _____ vertices.

2.

A rectangle has _____ straight sides.

A rectangle has _____ vertices.

3. Draw a shape with more than 4 vertices.

4. Draw a shape with more than 4 straight lines.

© Pearson Education, Inc. 1

Same Size and Same Shape

These rectangles are
the same shape.

These rectangles are
the same shape.

The rectangles are
the same size.
Count the dots to make sure.

The rectangles are **not**
the same size.
Count the dots to make sure.

Look at the first shape.
Then color the shape that matches it.

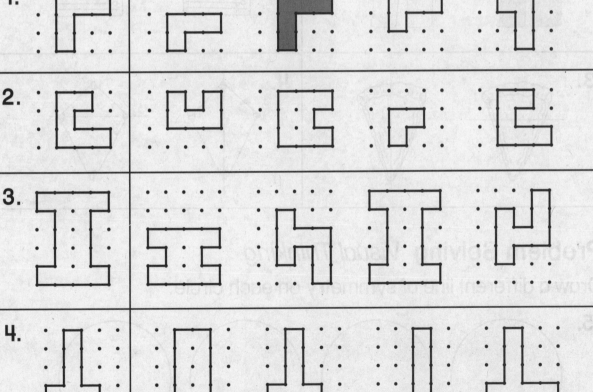

© Pearson Education, Inc. 1

Symmetry

A line of symmetry separates a shape into two matching parts.

These two parts match.

These two parts do not match.

Color the shape that has two matching parts.

1.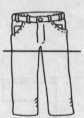

2.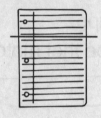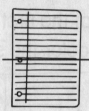

3.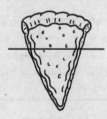

4.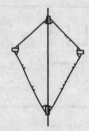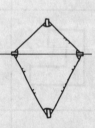

Problem Solving *Visual Thinking*

Draw a different line of symmetry on each circle.

5.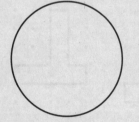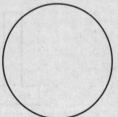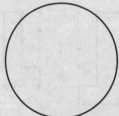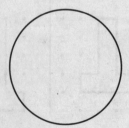

© Pearson Education, Inc. 1

Slides, Flips, and Turns

Shapes can slide.	Shapes can flip.	Shapes can turn.
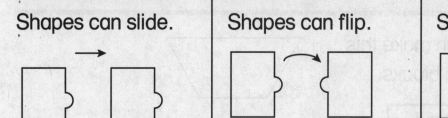		

Is it a **slide**, a **flip**, or a **turn**?
Circle the answer.

1.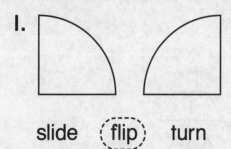

    slide   (flip)   turn

2.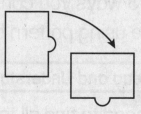

    slide   flip   turn

3.

    slide   flip   turn

4.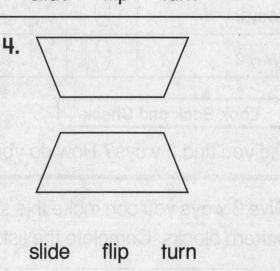

    slide   flip   turn

© Pearson Education, Inc. 1

Use with Lesson 5-8. **55**

Make an Organized List

Give 3 ways you can make this
shape using pattern blocks.

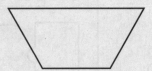

┌─────────────────────────────────┐
│ **Read and Understand** │
└─────────────────────────────────┘

You need to find all the ways that pattern blocks can make the shape.

┌─────────────────────────────────┐
│ **Plan and Solve** │
└─────────────────────────────────┘

A list can help you keep track.

Ways to Make ▽			
Shapes I Used	⬠	△	▱
Way 1	1	0	0
Way 2	0	3	0
Way 3	0	1	1

┌─────────────────────────────────┐
│ **Look Back and Check** │
└─────────────────────────────────┘

Did you find 3 ways? How do you know?

Give 3 ways you can make this shape using
pattern blocks. Complete the list.

I.

Ways to Make ▱			
Shapes I Used	⬠	▱	△
Way 1	1	0	1
Way 2			
Way 3			

© Pearson Education, Inc. 1

Equal Parts

This apple pie is divided into equal parts.

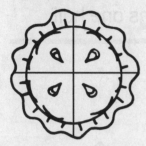

Each part is the same size.

There are __4__ equal parts.

This apple pie is **not** divided into equal parts.

Each part is **not** the same size.

There are __0__ equal parts.

Write the number of equal parts on each shape.

1.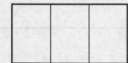

There are __3__ equal parts.

2.

There are _____ equal parts.

3.

There are _____ equal parts.

4.

There are _____ equal parts.

5.

There are _____ equal parts.

6.

There are _____ equal parts.

© Pearson Education, Inc. 1

Halves

This rectangle has 2 equal parts.
Each part is one half of the rectangle.
$\frac{1}{2}$ is a fraction that means one half.

Circle the shape that shows halves.
Color one half.

1.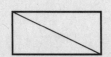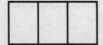

2.

3.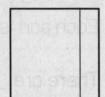

4.

5.

6.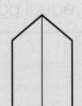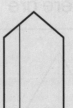

© Pearson Education, Inc. 1

Thirds and Fourths

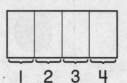

There are 3 **equal** parts.
Each part is one third, or
$\frac{1}{3}$, of the rectangle.

There are 4 **equal** parts.
Each part is one fourth, or
$\frac{1}{4}$, of the rectangle.

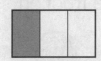 $\frac{1}{3}$ is shaded.

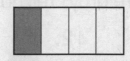 $\frac{1}{4}$ is shaded.

---

1. Circle the shape that
   shows one third shaded.

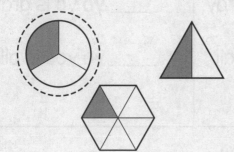

2. Circle the shape that
   shows one fourth shaded.

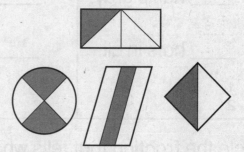

Circle the fraction that shows the shaded part.

3.

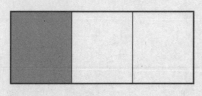

$\frac{1}{3}$ $\frac{1}{4}$

4.

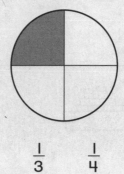

$\frac{1}{3}$ $\frac{1}{4}$

© Pearson Education, Inc. 1

Fractions of a Set

1 ball is gray.
2 balls in all.
$\frac{1}{2}$ of the balls are gray.

1 ball is gray.
3 balls in all.
$\frac{1}{3}$ of the balls are gray.

1 ball is gray.
4 balls in all.
$\frac{1}{4}$ of the balls are gray.

Tell how many are gray. Tell how many in all. Circle the fraction.

1.

____ hat is gray.

____ hats in all.

$\frac{1}{2}$ $\frac{1}{3}$ $\left(\frac{1}{4}\right)$

2.

____ doll is gray.

____ dolls in all.

$\frac{1}{2}$ $\frac{1}{3}$ $\frac{1}{4}$

3.

____ yo yo is gray.

____ yo yos in all.

$\frac{1}{2}$ $\frac{1}{3}$ $\frac{1}{4}$

Circle the fraction that tells what part of the group is gray.

4.

$\frac{1}{2}$ $\frac{1}{3}$ $\frac{1}{4}$

5.

$\frac{1}{2}$ $\frac{1}{3}$ $\frac{1}{4}$

6.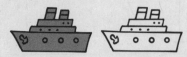

$\frac{1}{2}$ $\frac{1}{3}$ $\frac{1}{4}$

7.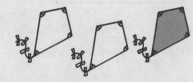

$\frac{1}{2}$ $\frac{1}{3}$ $\frac{1}{4}$

© Pearson Education, Inc. 1

Name _____

Non-Unit Fractions

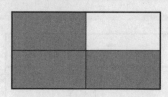 3 parts gray. 4 parts in all.
3 of 4 parts are gray.
$\frac{3}{4}$ of the shape is gray.

   3 shapes gray. 4 shapes in all.
3 of 4 shapes are gray.
$\frac{3}{4}$ of the shapes are gray.

Tell how many are gray. Write the fraction.

1.

___2___ of ___3___ cars are gray.

$\frac{2}{3}$ of the cars are gray.

2.

_____ of _____ parts are gray.

□/□ of the shape is gray.

Write the fraction that names the gray part.

3.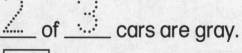

4.

5.

6.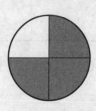

© Pearson Education, Inc. 1

Use Data from a Chart

How can you give an equal share of plums to each of 6 children?

The chart shows that there are 6 plums.

Use 6 counters.

	José	Juan	Sol
First give one counter to each child.	◯	◯	◯
Then give one more to each child.	◯	◯	◯

Fruit		
apples	🍎	12
bananas	🍌	8
oranges	🍊	9
plums	🍑	⑥

Each child gets __2__ plums.

Use the chart and counters to solve.
Draw equal shares.

1.

4 children want bananas.

Each child gets __2__ bananas.

2.

3 children want oranges.

Each child gets _____ oranges.

© Pearson Education, Inc. 1

Name _____

Shapes All Around Us

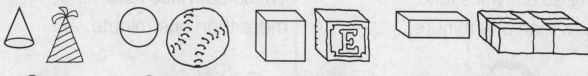

Cone   Sphere   Cube   Rectangular Prism

Find the solids in the picture.
Color the cones red. Color the spheres blue.
Color the cubes green. Color the rectangular prisms yellow.

1. How many cubes did you find? __6__

2. How many spheres did you find? _____

3. How many cones did you find? _____

4. How many rectangular prisms did you find? _____

5. Write a number sentence to tell how many
   more cubes there are than spheres.

_____ − _____ = _____ more cube

© Pearson Education, Inc. 1

Minutes

These activities take less than one minute.	These activities take more than one minute.

Does the activity take more or less than a minute?

Circle **more** or **less**.

1.

more   (less)

2.

more   less

3.

more   less

4.

more   less

© Pearson Education, Inc. **1**

Understanding the Hour and Minute Hands

The hour hand points to the 6.

The minute hand points to the 12.

When the minute hand points to 12, say o'clock.

hour hand __6__

minute hand __12__

__6__ o'clock

Write the time shown on each clock.

1.    hour hand __3__

minute hand __12__

__3__ o'clock

2.    hour hand _____

minute hand _____

_____ o'clock

3.    hour hand _____

minute hand _____

_____ o'clock

4.    hour hand _____

minute hand _____

_____ o'clock

Problem Solving *Mental Math*

Write the times that come next.

5. 4 o'clock   5 o'clock   _____ o'clock

6. 9 o'clock   10 o'clock   _____ o'clock

© Pearson Education, Inc. 1

Telling and Writing Time to the Hour

Both clocks show 4 o'clock.

4 tells the hour and...

...00 tells the minutes

The clocks show the same time.

Draw lines to match the clocks that show the same time.

1.

2.

3.

4.

© Pearson Education, Inc. 1

Name _____

Telling and Writing Time to the Half Hour

When it is 7:30, the hour hand will be halfway between

__7__ and __8__.

The minute hand

will be on __6__.

The hour hand is shorter than the minute hand.

Complete each sentence.

Then draw the hands on the clock face.

1.

The hour hand will be halfway

between __3__ and __4__.
The minute hand will

be on __6__.

2.

The hour hand will be halfway

between _____ and _____.
The minute hand will

be on _____.

3.

The hour hand will be halfway

between _____ and _____.
The minute hand will

be on _____.

© Pearson Education, Inc. 1

PROBLEM-SOLVING STRATEGY
Act It Out

The game starts at 3:00. It lasts 1 hour. When does it end?

Read and Understand

You need to find what time it will be 1 hour after 3 o'clock.

Plan and Solve

Show 3 o'clock.   Move the minute hand   One hour later
around the clock one time.

 3 o'clock ⟶ 1 hour ⟶ 4 o'clock

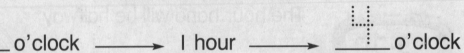

Write the ending time. Draw the hands on the clock.

1.

 ____ o'clock ⟶ 1 hour ⟶ ____ o'clock

2.

 ____ o'clock ⟶ 2 hours ⟶ ____ o'clock

© Pearson Education, Inc. 1

Ordering Events

You do things at different times of the day.

morning **afternoon** **night**

When did each of these things happen?
Write **morning**, **afternoon**, or **night** on the line.

1.

_____ _____ _____

2.

_____ _____ _____

© Pearson Education, Inc. 1

Name _____

Estimating Lengths of Time

About how long does each activity take?
You can estimate to find the answer.

(I minute)   I minute   I minute
I hour   (I hour)   I hour
I day   I day   (I day)

About how long does each activity take?
Circle your estimate.

1.
Do homework.

about I minute
(about I hour)
about I day

2.
Wash hands.

about I minute
about I hour
about I day

3.
Build a doghouse.

about I minute
about I hour
about I day

4.
Play a game.

about I minute
about I hour
about I day

© Pearson Education, Inc. 1

PROBLEM-SOLVING SKILL   R 6-8

Use Data from a Schedule

Nature Center Schedule	
Activity	**Time**
🚶 Hike	9:00
🐢 Feed Turtles	10:00
🌸 Pick Flowers	11:00
🐤 Bird Watch	12:00

A schedule tells the time at which activities start.

Look for the activity.

The hike starts at 9:00.

Look at the time.

At 12:00 we bird watch.

Use the schedule to answer the questions.
Circle your answer.

1. Which activity comes just before feeding the turtles?

    Bird Watch   Hike   Pick Flowers

2. Which activity comes just after picking flowers?

    Hike   Feed Turtles   Bird Watch

3. What time does the activity, Pick Flowers, begin?

    9:00   10:00   11:00

4. Which activity starts at 10:00?

    Hike   Feed Turtles   Bird Watch

© Pearson Education, Inc. 1

Days of the Week

March

	1st day	2nd day	3rd day	4th day	5th day	6th day	7th day
There are 7 days in a week.	Sunday	Monday	Tuesday	Wednesday	Thursday	Friday	Saturday
			1	2	3	4	5
	6	7	8	9	10	11	12
	13	14	15	16	17	18	19
	20	21	22	23	24	25	26
	27	28	29	30	31		

Use the calendar to answer the questions.

1. Write the days of the week in order.

   Sunday, __Monday__, Tuesday, _____,

   Thursday, _____, _____

2. Color all the Saturdays yellow. [| | | yellow ⊐]

3. Color all the Mondays blue. [| | | blue ⊐]

Problem Solving *Visual Thinking*

4. Find the pattern.

   Then write the day of the week that comes next.

   Wednesday, Thursday, _____, Saturday

5. Monday, Tuesday, _____, Thursday

© Pearson Education, Inc. 1

Months of the Year

> January is the first month of the year.

> February is the month **before** March.

> **March** is the third month.

> April is the month **after** March.

January						
S	M	T	W	T	F	S
				1	2	3
4	5	6	7	8	9	10
11	12	13	14	15	16	17
18	19	20	21	22	23	24
25	26	27	28	29	30	31

February						
S	M	T	W	T	F	S
1	2	3	4	5	6	7
8	9	10	11	12	13	14
15	16	17	18	19	20	21
22	23	24	25	26	27	28

March						
S	M	T	W	T	F	S
1	2	3	4	5	6	7
8	9	10	11	12	13	14
15	16	17	18	19	20	21
22	23	24	25	26	27	28
29	30	31				

April						
S	M	T	W	T	F	S
			1	2	3	4
5	6	7	8	9	10	11
12	13	14	15	16	17	18
19	20	21	22	23	24	25
26	27	28	29	30		

May						
S	M	T	W	T	F	S
					1	2
3	4	5	6	7	8	9
10	11	12	13	14	15	16
17	18	19	20	21	22	23
24/31	25	26	27	28	29	30

June						
S	M	T	W	T	F	S
	1	2	3	4	5	6
7	8	9	10	11	12	13
14	15	16	17	18	19	20
21	22	23	24	25	26	27
28	29	30				

July						
S	M	T	W	T	F	S
			1	2	3	4
5	6	7	8	9	10	11
12	13	14	15	16	17	18
19	20	21	22	23	24	25
26	27	28	29	30	31	

August						
S	M	T	W	T	F	S
						1
2	3	4	5	6	7	8
9	10	11	12	13	14	15
16	17	18	19	20	21	22
23/30	24/31	25	26	27	28	29

September						
S	M	T	W	T	F	S
		1	2	3	4	5
6	7	8	9	10	11	12
13	14	15	16	17	18	19
20	21	22	23	24	25	26
27	28	29	30			

October						
S	M	T	W	T	F	S
				1	2	3
4	5	6	7	8	9	10
11	12	13	14	15	16	17
18	19	20	21	22	23	24
25	26	27	28	29	30	31

November						
S	M	T	W	T	F	S
1	2	3	4	5	6	7
8	9	10	11	12	13	14
15	16	17	18	19	20	21
22	23	24	25	26	27	28
29	30					

December						
S	M	T	W	T	F	S
		1	2	3	4	5
6	7	8	9	10	11	12
13	14	15	16	17	18	19
20	21	22	23	24	25	26
27	28	29	30	31		

Use the calendar to answer the questions.

1. What are the names of the months?

   January, February, _____March_____, April, May,

   _____, July, August, _____,

   October, November, _____

2. Count the months. How many months are in a year? _____

3. Which month is the first month of the year? _____

4. Which month comes after May? _____

5. Which month comes before September? _____

© Pearson Education, Inc. 1

PROBLEM-SOLVING APPLICATIONS
What's Inside the Egg?

1. Jane uses a telescope to look at the birds.

What shape is the telescope?

cylinder

2. At 3 o'clock Jane sees a baby bird.
   Write the time on both clocks.

_____

3. On Monday 1 bird egg hatches.
   The next day 2 bird eggs hatch.
   On what day do the 2 bird eggs hatch?   _____

Writing in Math

4. It is April. In 2 months Jane will
   get a pet bird for her birthday.
   In what month is Jane's birthday?   _____

© Pearson Education, Inc. 1

Numbers to 19

Use counters and Workmat 3.
Write each number as 10 and some left over.

This shows 10.

 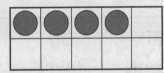

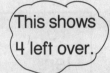
This shows 4 left over.

14 is 10 and 4.

1.

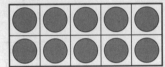 

17 is 10 and 7.

2.

16 is _____ and 6.

3.

15 is _____ and _____.

4.

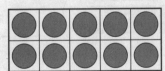 

18 is _____ and _____.

© Pearson Education, Inc. 1

Counting by 10s to 100

 stands for one group of ten.

10,	20,	30,	40,	50,
ten,	twenty,	thirty,	forty,	fifty,
60,	70,	80,	90,	100,
sixty,	seventy,	eighty,	ninety,	one hundred

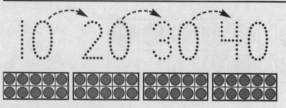

10 20 30 40

4 groups of ten

40 forty

Count by 10s. Then write the numbers.

1. 10 20 30 40 50

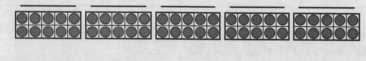

5 groups of ten

fifty

2.

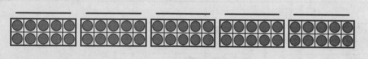

_____ groups of ten

_____ _____

3.

_____ groups of ten

_____ _____

© Pearson Education, Inc. 1

Use the hundred chart.
Count on from 24.

> Start at 24.
> Count on by 1s.

1	2	3	4	5	6	7	8	9	10
11	12	13	14	15	16	17	18	19	20
21	22	23	(24)	25	26	27	28	29	30
31	32	33	34	35	36	37	38	39	40
41	42	43	44	45	46	47	48	49	50
51	52	53	(54)	55	56	57	58	59	60
61	62	63	64	65	66	67	68	69	70
71	72	73	74	75	76	77	78	79	80
81	82	83	84	85	86	87	88	89	90
91	92	93	94	95	96	97	98	99	100

24, _25_, _26_, _27_

Count back from 54.

> Start at 54.
> Count back
> by 1s.

54, _53_, _52_, _51_

Write the missing numbers. Look for patterns.

1.

41	42			46	47		
51	52	54	55			58	59
	63		66	67			70
	74	75		78			

Use the hundred chart to count back by 1s.

2. 29, _28_, _27_, 26 _____, _____, 23

3. 31, _30_, _____, _____, 27, _____, _____

© Pearson Education, Inc. 1

Counting with Groups of 10 and Leftovers

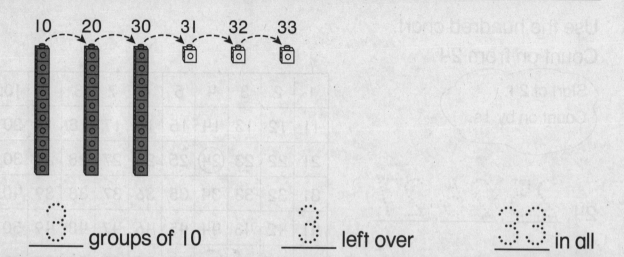

____3____ groups of 10   ____3____ left over   ░33░ in all

Use counters to show the snap cubes.
Make groups of 10.
Then write the numbers.

1. 10 20 21 22 23 24 25 26 27

____2____ groups of ten

____7____ left over

_____ in all

2.

_____ groups of ten

_____ left over

_____ in all

© Pearson Education, Inc. 1

Estimating with Groups of 10

An estimate tells **about** how many.

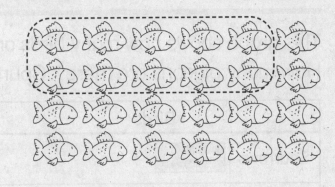

Circle 10 fish.
About how many more groups
of 10 fish do you see?

There are about   10   (20)   30   fish in all.

Circle a group of 10. Then circle the best estimate
for how many there are in all.

1.

about   10   (30)   50

2.

about   10   20   30

© Pearson Education, Inc. 1

PROBLEM-SOLVING SKILL   R 7-6

Use Data from a Graph

This graph shows how many birds are in the park.

How many pigeons are there? Count by 10s.

Birds			
Sparrows	⬛⬛⬛⬛⬛		
Pigeons	⬛⬛⬛⬛⬛	⬛⬛⬛⬛⬛	⬛⬛⬛⬛⬛
Robins	⬛⬛⬛⬛⬛	⬛⬛⬛⬛⬛	

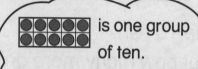 is one group of ten.
Count by 10s when there is more than one group.

There are __3__ groups of 10.

There are __30__ pigeons.

Use the graph to answer each question.

1. How many sparrows are there?

   There is __1__ group of 10.

   There are _____ sparrows.

2. Of which kind of bird is
   there the most?

   _____

3. How many pigeons and
   robins are there altogether?   _____

4. How many more pigeons than
   sparrows are there?   _____

© Pearson Education, Inc. 1

Skip-Counting Patterns on the Hundred Chart

Skip count by 10s on the hundred chart.

1	2	3	4	5	6	7	8	9	10		10
11	12	13	14	15	16	17	18	19	20		20
21	22	23	24	25	26	27	28	29	30		30
31	32	33	34	35	36	37	38	39	40		40
41	42	43	44	45	46	47	48	49	50		50
51	52	53	54	55	56	57	58	59	60		60
61	62	63	64	65	66	67	68	69	70		70
71	72	73	74	75	76	77	78	79	80		80
81	82	83	84	85	86	87	88	89	90		90
91	92	93	94	95	96	97	98	99	100		100

When you skip count by 10s all of the numbers end in 0.

1. Skip count by 5s. Draw a square around the numbers you say.

2. When you skip count by 5s, all of the numbers end in

_____ or _____.

1	2	3	4	5	6	7	8	9	10
11	12	13	14	15	16	17	18	19	20
21	22	23	24	25	26	27	28	29	30
31	32	33	34	35	36	37	38	39	40
41	42	43	44	45	46	47	48	49	50
51	52	53	54	55	56	57	58	59	60
61	62	63	64	65	66	67	68	69	70
71	72	73	74	75	76	77	78	79	80
81	82	83	84	85	86	87	88	89	90
91	92	93	94	95	96	97	98	99	100

© Pearson Education, Inc. 1

Using Skip Counting

Skip count to find how many.

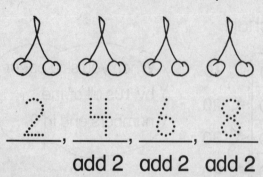

> Skip count by 2, or add 2 to the last number.

2, 4, 6, 8
    add 2 add 2 add 2

There are ___8___ cherries.

I. Skip count by 2s.

___2___, ___4___, _____, _____, _____, _____

---

2. Skip count by 5s.

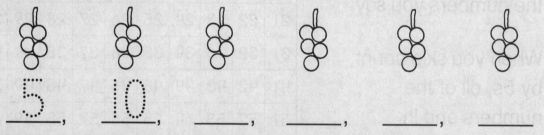

___5___, ___10___, _____, _____, _____, _____

---

3. Skip count by 10s.

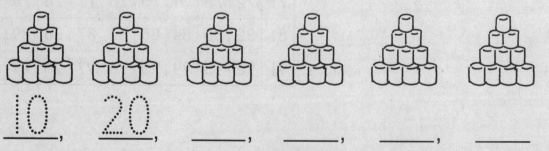

___10___, ___20___, _____, _____, _____, _____

© Pearson Education, Inc. 1

Look for a Pattern

The children need mittens.

Each child has two hands.

How many mittens are needed for all of the children?

Read and Understand

You need to find how many hands the children have altogether.

Plan and Solve

Make a table to show a pattern. Write the numbers.

Count the children by 1s.

Count the mittens by 2s.

Number of Children	1	2		
Number of Mittens	2	4		

8 mittens will be needed for all of the children.

Look Back and Check

Does your answer make sense?

Find the pattern. Write the numbers.

1. There are 4 boxes.
   Each box has 5 crayons.
   How many crayons are
   there in all?

Number of Boxes	1	2		
Number of Crayons	5			

There are _____ crayons in all.

© Pearson Education, Inc. 1

Before, After, and Between

First find 34 on the chart.

1	2	3	4	5	6	7	8	9	10
11	12	13	14	15	16	17	18	19	20
21	22	23	24	25	26	27	28	29	30
31	32	33	34	35	36	37	38	39	40
41	42	43	44	45	46	47	48	49	50

Look to the left of 34 to find the number that comes before it.

33 comes **before** 34.

Look to the right of 34 to find the number that comes after it.

35 comes **after** 34.

34 comes **between** 33 and 35.

Use Workmat 6 if you like.

Write the number that comes before.

1. 23 , 24   _____, 47   _____, 19

Write the number that comes after.

2. 32, 33   41, _____   27, _____

Write the number that comes between.

3. 22, _____, 24   45, _____, 47   32, _____, 34

Problem Solving *Reasoning*

Write the number that answers the riddle.

4. I am a number between 10 and 20.

    You say my name when you count by 5s.

    What number am I? _____

© Pearson Education, Inc. 1

Odd and Even Numbers

6 is an even number.
It makes equal rows.
There are no extras.

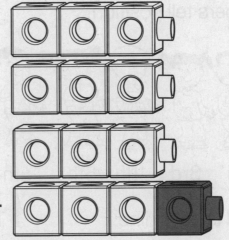

These cubes match.

7 is an odd number.
It does not make equal rows.
There is 1 extra.

These cubes don't match.

Use cubes to show each number.
Try to make equal rows.
Then circle **odd** or **even**.

1.

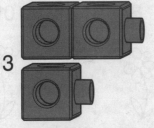

3

(odd)

even

2.

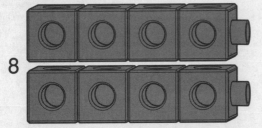

8

odd

even

3.

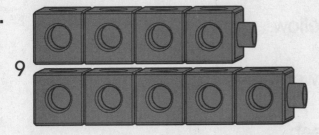

9

odd

even

© Pearson Education, Inc. 1

Ordinal Numbers Through Twentieth

Ordinal numbers tell position.

| 1st | 2nd | 3rd | 4th | 5th | 6th | 7th | 8th | 9th | 10th |

↑ This girl is 1st in line.   ↑ This boy is 6th in line.

Follow the directions to show the position of the flowers.

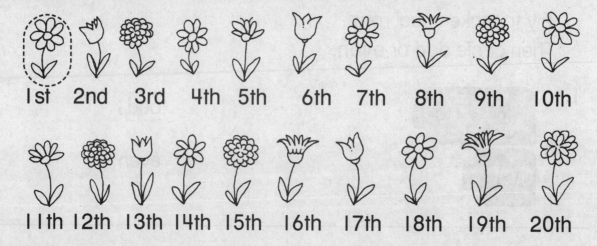

| 1st | 2nd | 3rd | 4th | 5th | 6th | 7th | 8th | 9th | 10th |

| 11th | 12th | 13th | 14th | 15th | 16th | 17th | 18th | 19th | 20th |

1. Circle the 1st flower in blue.

2. Circle the 10th flower in red.

3. Cross out the 18th flower.

4. Circle the 12th flower in yellow.

5. Draw a box around the flower that is 15th.

6. Circle the 5th flower in green.

86 Use with Lesson 7-12.

© Pearson Education, Inc. 1

PROBLEM-SOLVING APPLICATIONS

By the Sea

You can skip count to find out how many.

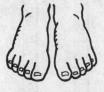 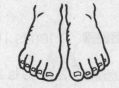 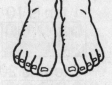

How many toes? Skip count by fives.
Add 5 to each number to get the next number.

5, 10, 15, 20, 25, 30

I. Each boat has 2 sails. If there are 5 boats in all, skip count
to find how many sails there are.

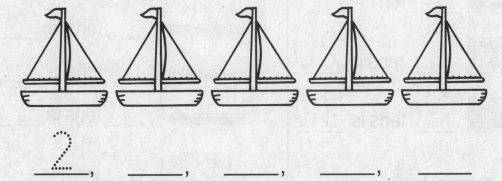

2, _____, _____, _____, _____

2. Is there an odd or even number of boats?

odd   even

3.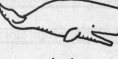

4th   3rd   2nd   1st

Circle the 1st whale.
Color the 3rd whale blue.

© Pearson Education, Inc. 1

Numbers Made with Tens

You can count the models to find out
how many groups of ten.

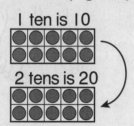

1 ten is 10

2 tens is 20

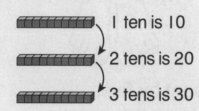

1 ten is 10

2 tens is 20

3 tens is 30

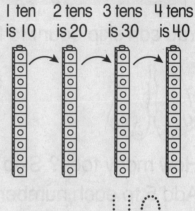

| 1 ten is 10 | 2 tens is 20 | 3 tens is 30 | 4 tens is 40 |

2 tens is _20_.   3 tens is _30_.   4 tens is _40_.

Count the models. Write how many. Then write the number.

1.

_1_ ten is _10_

_2_ tens is _20_

_3_ tens is _30_

_3_ tens is _30_.

2.

_____ ten is _____

_____ tens is _____

_____ tens is _____

_____ tens is _____

_4_ tens is _____.

3.

_____ ten is _____

_____ tens is _____

_____ tens is _____

_____ tens is _____

_____ tens is _____

_____ tens is _____.

© Pearson Education, Inc. 1

Tens and Ones

Here are some ways you can show a number.

Tens	Ones
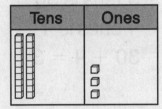	

Tens	Ones
2	3

2 tens 3 ones

23

2 tens 3 ones

23

2 tens 3 ones

23

Count the tens and ones. Then write the numbers.

1.

Tens	Ones

Tens	Ones
3	*2*

__*3*__ tens __*2*__ ones

32

__*3*__ tens __*2*__ ones

32

__*32*__

2.

Tens	Ones

Tens	Ones

_____ tens _____ ones

_____

_____ tens _____ ones

_____

_____

© Pearson Education, Inc. 1

Modeling Numbers and Expanded Form R 8-3

The chart shows

Tens	Ones

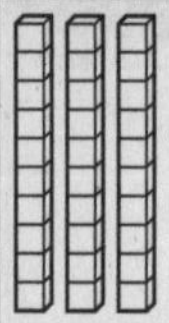

3 tens is 30
4 ones is 4
30 + 4 = 34

34 is the same as 3 tens and 4 ones.

3 tens   4 ones

Count the tens and ones. Then write the numbers.

I.

Tens 	Ones 

__2__ tens and __4__ ones

__2__ tens is __20__
__4__ ones is __4__
__20__ + __4__ = __24__

2.

Tens 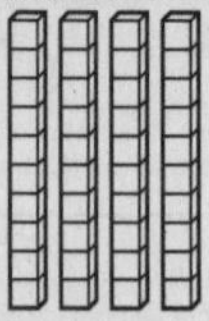	Ones 

_____ tens and _____ ones

_____ tens is _____
_____ ones is _____
_____ + _____ = _____

3.

Tens 	Ones 

_____ tens and _____ ones

_____ tens is _____
_____ ones is _____
_____ + _____ = _____

© Pearson Education, Inc. 1

Name _____

Ways to Make Numbers

R 8-4

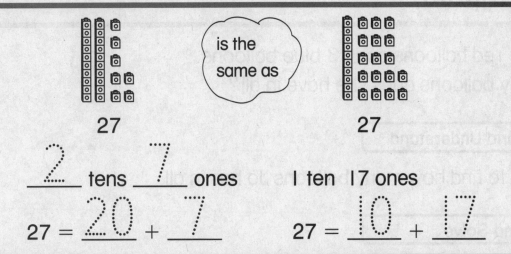

is the same as

27   27

__2__ tens __7__ ones   I ten I7 ones

27 = __20__ + __7__   27 = __10__ + __17__

Use cubes and Workmat 4 to show a different way to make the number. Draw the ones.

I.   32

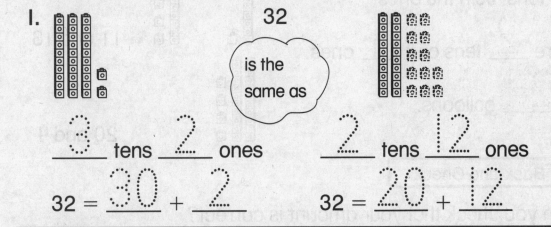

is the same as

__3__ tens __2__ ones   __2__ tens __I2__ ones

32 = __30__ + __2__   32 = __20__ + __I2__

2.

is the same as

_____ tens _____ ones   _____ tens _____ ones

43 = _____ + _____   43 = _____ + _____

© Pearson Education, Inc. 1

Use with Lesson 8-4. **91**

Name _____

PROBLEM-SOLVING STRATEGY

Use Objects

Jo has 11 red balloons and 13 blue balloons.
How many balloons does she have in all?

Read and Understand

You need to find how many balloons Jo has in all.

Plan and Solve

Make each number with cubes.

Put the cubes together.
Join the tens. Join the ones.

There are __2__ tens and __4__ ones.

Jo has __24__ balloons.

11 and 13

is

20 and 4

Look Back and Check

How can you check that your amount is correct?

Use cubes to find how many in all.

1. Dan has 22 books. Mike has 13 books.
   How many books do they have in all?

   There are _____ tens and _____ ones.

   They have _____ books in all.

© Pearson Education, Inc. 1

1 More, 1 Less;
10 More, 10 Less

34 take away 10 is 24.

10 less than 34 is **24**.

34 and 10 more is 44.

10 more than 34 is **44**.

Use cubes. Write the numbers.

1.

23 take away 1 is **22**.

1 less than 23 is _____.

23 and 1 more is **24**.

1 more than 23 is _____.

2.

1 less than 45 is _____.

1 more than 45 is _____.

3.

10 less than 68 is _____.

10 more than 68 is _____.

© Pearson Education, Inc. 1

Name _____

Comparing Numbers: Greater Than, Less Than, Equal

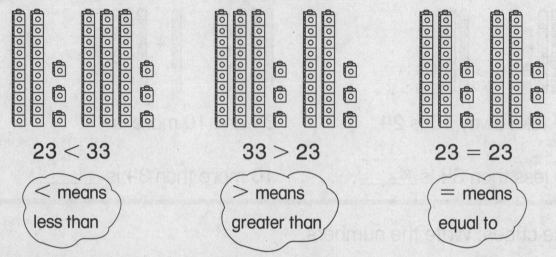

$23 < 33$ $33 > 23$ $23 = 23$

$<$ means less than

$>$ means greater than

$=$ means equal to

23 is **less than** 33   33 is **greater than** 23   23 is **equal to** 23

Circle **less than**, **greater than**, or **equal to**.

Write $<$, $>$, or $=$.

1. 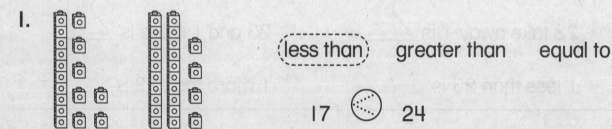   (less than)   greater than   equal to

17 ⬤ 24

2. 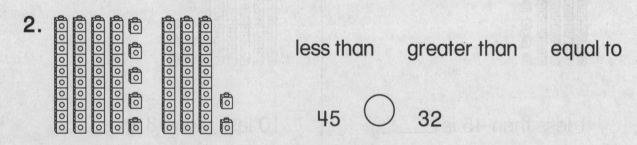   less than   greater than   equal to

45 ◯ 32

3. 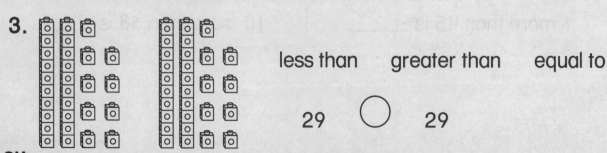   less than   greater than   equal to

29 ◯ 29

© Pearson Education, Inc. 1

Number-Line Estimation: Numbers to 100

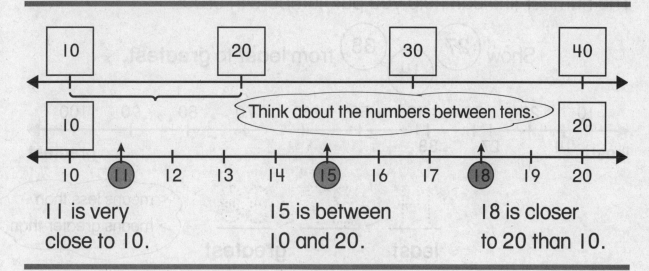

10   20   30   40

Think about the numbers between tens.

10   20

10 11 12 13 14 15 16 17 18 19 20

11 is very
close to 10.

15 is between
10 and 20.

18 is closer
to 20 than 10.

Count by tens to complete the number line.
Then draw lines to show where the numbers go.

1.

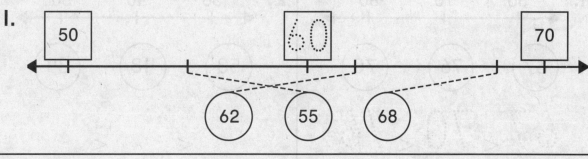

50   60   70

62   55   68

2.

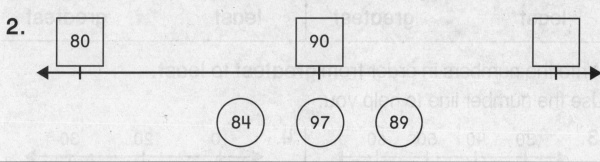

80   90

84   97   89

3.

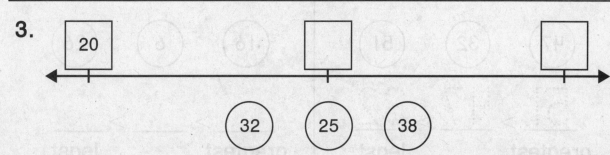

20

32   25   38

© Pearson Education, Inc. 1

Ordering Three Numbers

The number line can help you put numbers in order.

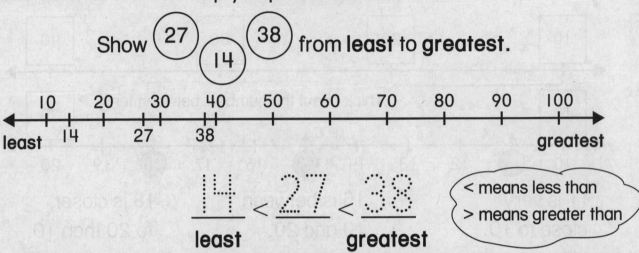

Show (27) (14) (38) from **least** to **greatest**.

$$\underset{\text{least}}{14} < \underset{}{27} < \underset{\text{greatest}}{38}$$

< means less than
> means greater than

Write the numbers in order from **least** to **greatest**.

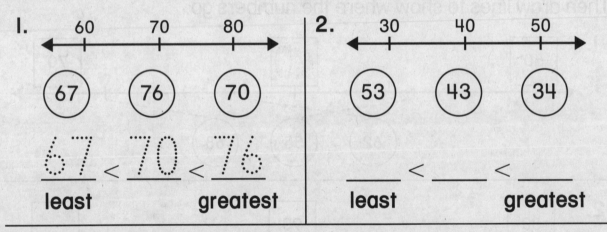

1.

(67) (76) (70)

$$\underset{\text{least}}{67} < \underset{}{70} < \underset{\text{greatest}}{76}$$

2.

(53) (43) (34)

$$\underset{\text{least}}{\underline{}} < \underline{} < \underset{\text{greatest}}{\underline{}}$$

Write the numbers in order from **greatest** to **least**.
Use the number line to help you.

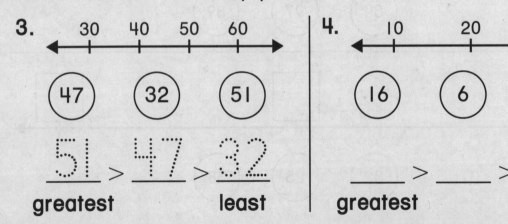

3.

(47) (32) (51)

$$\underset{\text{greatest}}{51} > \underset{}{47} > \underset{\text{least}}{32}$$

4.

(16) (6) (26)

$$\underset{\text{greatest}}{\underline{}} > \underline{} > \underset{\text{least}}{\underline{}}$$

© Pearson Education, Inc. 1

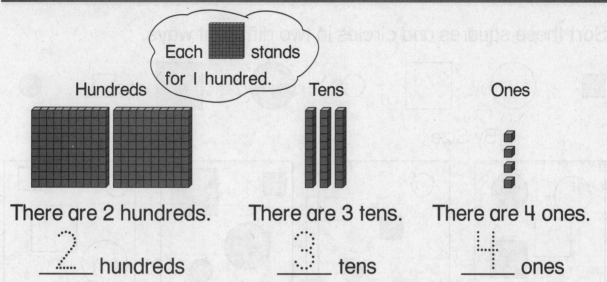

Each ▨ stands for 1 hundred.

Hundreds   Tens   Ones

There are 2 hundreds.   There are 3 tens.   There are 4 ones.

__2__ hundreds   __3__ tens   __4__ ones

234

Write how many hundreds, tens, and ones there are.
Then write the number.

1.

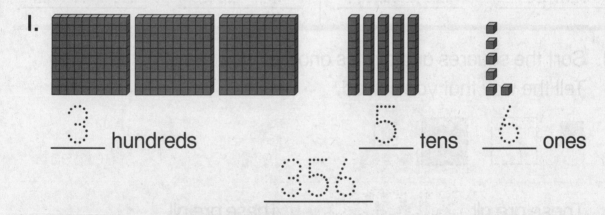

__3__ hundreds   __5__ tens   __6__ ones

__356__

2.

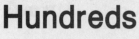

_____ hundreds   _____ tens   _____ ones

_____

© Pearson Education, Inc. 1

Sorting

Sort these squares and circles in two different ways.

By Size		By Color	
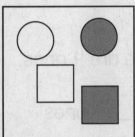	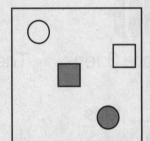	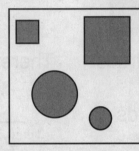	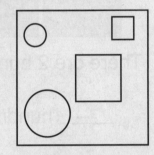
These squares and circles are **big**.	These squares and circles are **small**.	These squares and circles are **gray**.	These squares and circles are **white**.

1. Sort the squares and circles another way.
   Tell the way that you sorted.

   These are all **squares**.   These are all _____.

   I sorted by _____.

Problem Solving *Reasoning*

2. Circle the shape that does not belong in the group.

© Pearson Education, Inc. 1

Making Graphs

Each flower is 1 selection.

Favorite Flower

✿ Daisy	✿	✿	✿	✿	✿	✿	✿		
❀ Tulip	❀	❀	❀	❀					

Count the pictures in the graph.

How many boxes have a daisy? ___7___

How many boxes have a tulip? ___4___

Which flower is the favorite? ___Daisy___

---

1. Ask your classmates to select their favorite drink.
   Draw to make a picture graph.

Our Favorite Drink

🍎 Apple Juice									
🥛 Milk									

2. What will you draw to show apple juice? ___🍎___

3. What will you draw to show milk? _____

4. How many children selected apple juice? _____

5. Which drink is the least favorite? _____

© Pearson Education, Inc. 1

Name _____

Making Bar Graphs

Each square that is colored gray equals 1 child's selection.

Our Favorite Fairy-Tale Character

Names of Fairy-Tale Characters

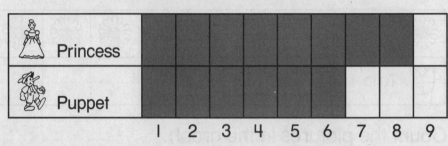

| | 1 | 2 | 3 | 4 | 5 | 6 | 7 | 8 | 9 |

Number of selections

Look at the number of squares colored for the princess.

How many squares are colored? __8__

Look at the number of squares colored for the puppet.

How many squares are colored? __6__

Circle the favorite fairy-tale character of the children.

(Princess)   Puppet

---

1. Ask your classmates to select their favorite snack.
   Color to make a bar graph. Then answer the questions.

Yogurt									
Fruit									
	1	2	3	4	5	6	7	8	9

2. Which snack is the favorite? _____

3. How many children selected fruit? _____

© Pearson Education, Inc. 1

Using Tally Marks

The children made tally marks to show the ways
children get to school.

| equals 1   (count 5 6 7)   𝗛𝗛𝗛 equals 5

		Total
Walk	𝗛𝗛𝗛 | |	7
School bus	𝗛𝗛𝗛 𝗛𝗛𝗛	10

(count 5   10)

---

1. Color some balloons red. Color the rest blue.
   Use tally marks to show how many balloons
   there are in each color. Write the totals.

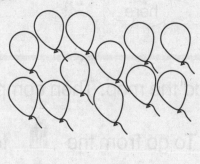

		Total
Red		
Blue		

Use the tally chart to answer the questions.

2. Of which color are there the most? _____

3. Of which color are there the fewest? _____

4. How many balloons are there altogether? _____

© Pearson Education, Inc. 1

Coordinate Grids

This is a map of Felipe's town.
You want to go from the school to Felipe's house.

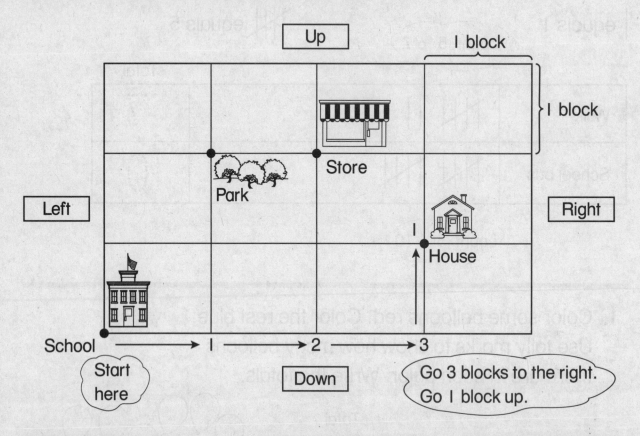

Read the map. Then complete each sentence.

1. To go from the 🏫 to the 🌳,

go __1__ block right and __2__ blocks up.

2. To go from the 🏠 to the 🏪 ,

go ___ block left and ___ block up.

3. To go from the 🏠 to the 🌳,

go ___ blocks left and ___ block up.

© Pearson Education, Inc. 1

PROBLEM-SOLVING SKILL
Use Data from a Map

This is a map of a neighborhood.
How many blocks is it from the house to the park?

Step 1:
You need to find out how many blocks in all.

Step 2:
Look at the map.
Find the house.
Find the park.

From house to store ___3___ blocks.

From store to park ___2___ blocks.

Step 3:
Write an addition sentence.

___3___ + ___2___ = ___5___ blocks

It is 5 blocks from the house to the park.

---

1. How many blocks is it from the park to the school?
   Find the shortest path. Write an addition sentence.

   From the 🌳🌳 to the 🏛 _____ blocks

   From the 🏛 to the 🏫 _____ blocks

   _____ + _____ = _____ blocks

© Pearson Education, Inc. 1

Let's Make Soup!

Count the striped fish. Make 1 tally mark for each striped fish. Count the dotted fish. Make 1 tally mark for each dotted fish. Write the totals.

Remember ||||| equals 5.

		Total
 striped fish	||||| |||	
dotted fish	||||| ||	

Look back and check.

Count the striped fish again. How many are there? __8__
Count the tally marks for striped fish.

What is the total? __8__

Are the numbers the same? __yes__

1. How many dotted fish did you count? _____

2. How many dotted fish are on the tally chart? _____

3. How many fewer dotted fish are there than striped fish? _____

4. Circle the picture that shows what you wrote on the tally chart.

  <    >

© Pearson Education, Inc. 1

Name _____

R 9-1

Nickel and Penny

A nickel = 5 cents.
Skip count by 5s for nickels.

A penny = I cent.
Count by I s for pennies.

Skip count by 5s for the nickels.
Then count on by I s for the pennies.

5¢ → 10¢ → 15¢ → 16¢ → 17¢ → 18¢   **In All** 18¢

Skip count by 5s and count on by I s to find
how much money in all.

I.

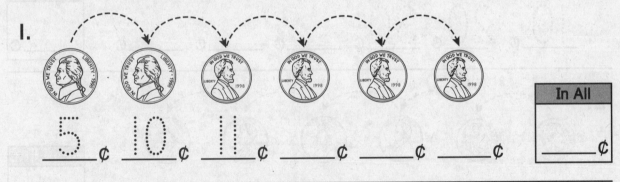

5¢ 10¢ 11¢ ___¢ ___¢ ___¢   **In All** ___¢

2.

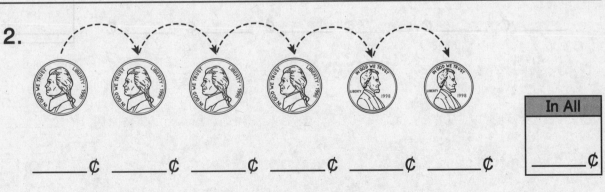

___¢ ___¢ ___¢ ___¢ ___¢ ___¢   **In All** ___¢

© Pearson Education, Inc. 1

Use with Lesson 9-1. **105**

Dime

A dime = 10 cents.
Skip count by 10s for dimes.

A penny = 1 cent.
Count by 1s for pennies.

Skip count by 10s. Then count on by 1s.

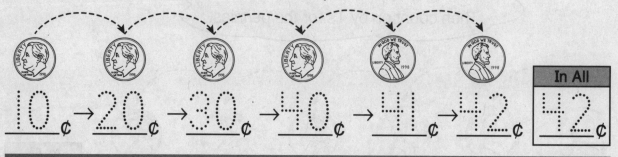

$10_¢ \rightarrow 20_¢ \rightarrow 30_¢ \rightarrow 40_¢ \rightarrow 41_¢ \rightarrow 42_¢$

In All
42¢

Skip count by 10s and count on by 1s to find
how much money in all.

1.

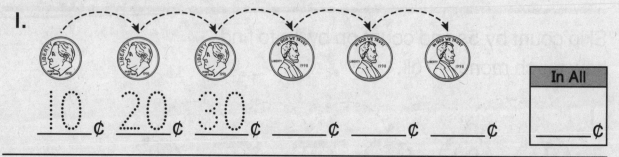

$10_¢ \quad 20_¢ \quad 30_¢ \quad \underline{\quad}_¢ \quad \underline{\quad}_¢ \quad \underline{\quad}_¢$

In All
____¢

2.

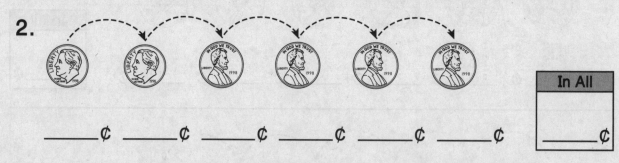

$\underline{\quad}_¢ \quad \underline{\quad}_¢ \quad \underline{\quad}_¢ \quad \underline{\quad}_¢ \quad \underline{\quad}_¢ \quad \underline{\quad}_¢$

In All
____¢

© Pearson Education, Inc. 1

Counting Dimes and Nickels

Count dimes by 10s.   Count nickels by 5s.

(Count the dimes first.)   (Then count the nickels.)

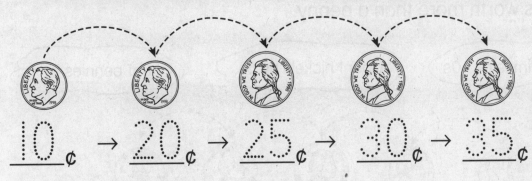

$\underline{10}_¢ \rightarrow \underline{20}_¢ \rightarrow \underline{25}_¢ \rightarrow \underline{30}_¢ \rightarrow \underline{35}_¢$

In All
$35_¢$

Count on. Then write how much money in all.

1.

$\underline{10}_¢ \quad \underline{15}_¢ \quad \underline{}_¢ \quad \underline{}_¢ \quad \underline{}_¢$

In All
_____ ¢

2.

$\underline{}_¢ \quad \underline{}_¢ \quad \underline{}_¢ \quad \underline{}_¢ \quad \underline{}_¢ \quad \underline{}_¢$

In All
_____ ¢

© Pearson Education, Inc. 1

Counting Dimes, Nickels, and Pennies

When you count coins, start with the coin that is
worth the most.

A dime is worth more than a nickel.
A nickel is worth more than a penny.

Count dimes by 10s.   Count nickels by 5s.   Count pennies by 1s.

10¢ → 20¢ → 30¢ → 35¢ → 40¢ → 41¢   **In All** 41¢

Count on. Then write how much money in all.

1.
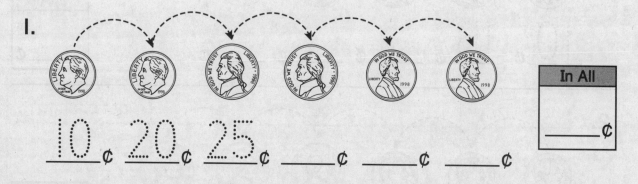

10¢ 20¢ 25¢ _____¢ _____¢ _____¢   **In All** _____¢

2.
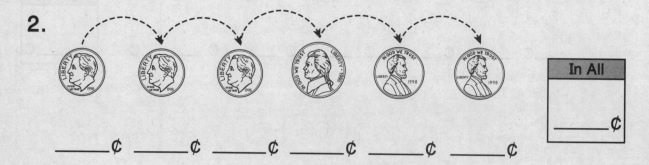

_____¢ _____¢ _____¢ _____¢ _____¢ _____¢   **In All** _____¢

© Pearson Education, Inc. 1

Use Data from a Table

Meg buys a top.
She gives the clerk a dime.
Will she get change?

Toys		
Top		9¢
Ball		7¢
Jacks		5¢

The price of the toy is on the same line as the toy.

Find the top in the table.
How much is a top?

A top is __9__ ¢.

Read the story again.
How much money did Meg give the clerk?

Meg gave the clerk __a dime__.

A dime is 10¢.

10¢ is more than 9¢.

Will Meg get change? __yes__

Use the table above. Circle **yes** or **no**.

You Buy	You Use	Will you get change?
1.		yes no
2.		yes no

© Pearson Education, Inc. 1

Quarter

There are different ways you can make 25 cents.

Skip count by 10s and then by 5s.

10¢ → 20¢ → 25¢   10¢ → 15¢ → 20¢ → 25¢

Count each group of coins.
Circle the group of coins in each row that equals 25 cents.

1.

2.

3.

Problem Solving *Visual Thinking*

4. Chris has 4 coins in her purse.
   They are worth 25¢ in all.
   Draw the other 2 coins.

© Pearson Education, Inc. 1

Counting Sets of Coins

 > > > (penny) (Remember > stands for greater than.)

Count the coins. Start with the coin that is worth the most money.

Count on by 10s.   Count on by 5s.   Count on by 1s.

$25_¢ \to 35_¢ \to 45_¢ \to 50_¢ \to 55_¢ \to 56_¢ \to 57_¢$

In All
57 ¢

Count on. Then write how much money in all.

I.

$25_¢$ $35_¢$ ____ ¢ ____ ¢ ____ ¢ ____ ¢

In All
____ ¢

2.

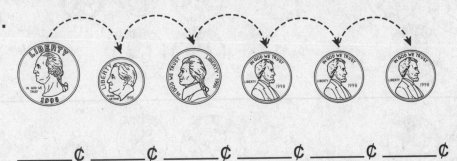

____ ¢ ____ ¢ ____ ¢ ____ ¢ ____ ¢ ____ ¢

In All
____ ¢

© Pearson Education, Inc. 1

Half-Dollar and Dollar

Here are some ways to show one dollar.

dollar bill	dollar coin

$1.00 = 100¢

 or

$1.00 = 100¢

half-dollar coin

 or

half-dollar = 50¢
2 half-dollars = 100¢

4 quarters

$25¢ → 50¢ → 75¢ → 100¢

4 quarters = 100¢

Circle the group of coins in each row that makes $1.00.

1.

2.

3.

© Pearson Education, Inc. 1

PROBLEM-SOLVING STRATEGY

Try, Check, and Revise

Jim bought 2 toys at the toy fair. Together they cost 11¢.
Which toys did he buy?

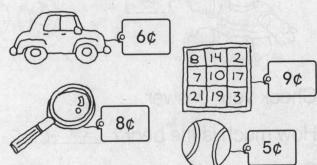

Read and Understand

Pick two toys. Find their total.

Plan and Solve

Try  and .

Add. __6__¢ + __8__¢ = __14__¢

14¢ is more than 11¢.

Find a toy that costs less than .

The costs less.

Try the  and .

Add. __6__¢ + __5__¢ = __11__¢

Jim bought the  and .

Look Back and Check

How can you check your answer?

1. Circle the 2 toys that cost 15¢.

____¢ + ____¢ = ____¢

© Pearson Education, Inc. 1

What Can You Buy?

8¢

Check your answer.

How much is the bear? __8__ ¢

Count the coins you circled.

How much are they worth? __8__ ¢

Do the coins equal the price of the bear? ___yes___

---

1. Circle the coins you need to buy 2 bears.

---

2. Is the price of the 2 bears
   an odd or even number? _____

---

3. Circle the coins you need to buy the puzzle.

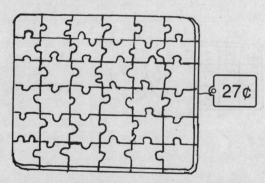
27¢

© Pearson Education, Inc. 1

Estimating, Measuring, and Comparing Length

Look at the paper clip.

Look at the string.

Estimate: How many paper clips long is the string?

About __5__ paper clips long.

Now measure.

> Be sure paper clips are all the same size.

> Be sure you put the paper clips right next to each other.

> Line up the first paper clip with the edge.

Measure: About __6__ paper clips long.

That is close to the estimate.

Estimate. Then measure using paper clips.

	Estimate.	Measure.
1.	about ____ ⊂⊐	____ ⊂⊐
2.	about ____ ⊂⊐	____ ⊂⊐
3.	about ____ ⊂⊐	____ ⊂⊐

© Pearson Education, Inc. 1

Name _____

PROBLEM-SOLVING STRATEGY

R 10-2

Use Logical Reasoning

Predict: Will you need more chalk or
more paper clips to measure the marker?

more or more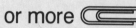

Read and Understand

You must find out if you need more chalk or more paper clips.

Plan and Solve

Use reasoning to help you.
The paper clip is shorter.
You will probably need more paper clips.

more 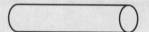   more

Measure to check.

about _8_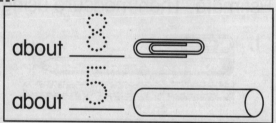

about _5_

Look Back and Check

Measure to check your prediction.
Was your prediction correct?

Will it take fewer pieces of chalk or fewer paper clips?
Circle your prediction. Then measure.

I.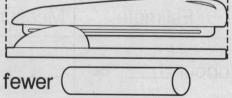

fewer

fewer

Measure to check.

about _____

about _____

© Pearson Education, Inc. 1

116 Use with Lesson 10-2.

Estimating and Measuring with Inches

This is 1 inch.

About how many inches long is this ribbon?

About __6__ inches long.
Measure. Use a ruler.

> Line up the edge of the ribbon with the edge of the ruler.

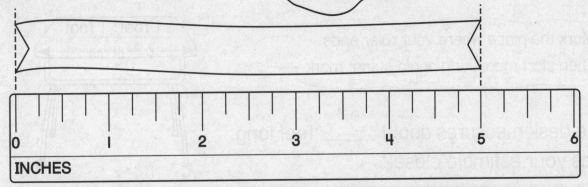

INCHES

The ribbon measures __5__ inches long.
Was your estimate correct?

Estimate the length. Then measure using a ruler.

1.

Estimate.

about _____ inches

Measure.

_____ inches

© Pearson Education, Inc. 1

Estimating and Measuring with Feet

A foot is 12 inches long.
This football is about 1 foot long.
An inch ruler is 1 foot long.

About how long is your desk?

about _____ feet long

You can use an inch ruler to measure the length of your desk.

Mark the place where your ruler ends.
Then start measuring again at that mark.

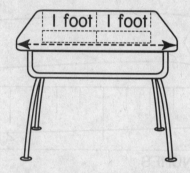

The desk measures about __2__ feet long.
Was your estimate close?

Find each object in your classroom.
Estimate. Then measure the length using a ruler.

1.

Estimate. about _____ feet long

Measure. about _____ feet long

2.

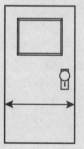

Estimate. about _____ feet long

Measure. about _____ feet long

© Pearson Education, Inc. 1

Estimating and Measuring with Centimeters

This is I centimeter high.

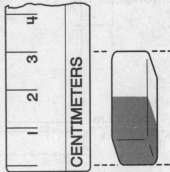

About how many centimeters high is this eraser?

The eraser is about __2__ centimeters high.
Use a centimeter ruler to measure the eraser.

> When you measure height, you measure up and down.

The eraser measures __3__ centimeters.
The estimate is close.

Estimate the height. Then measure using a centimeter ruler.

I.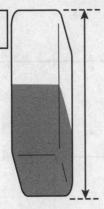

Estimate.

about _____ centimeters

Measure.

about _____ centimeters

2.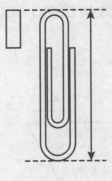

Estimate.

about _____ centimeters

Measure.

about _____ centimeters

3.

Estimate.

about _____ centimeters

Measure.

about _____ centimeters

4.

Estimate.

about _____ centimeters

Measure.

about _____ centimeters

© Pearson Education, Inc. 1

Understanding Perimeter

Count the inches around a shape to find the perimeter.

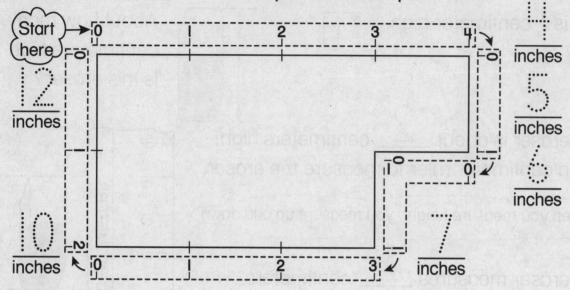

The perimeter of the shape is __12__ inches.

How many inches around each shape?

1.

The perimeter
of the triangle is _____ inches.

2.

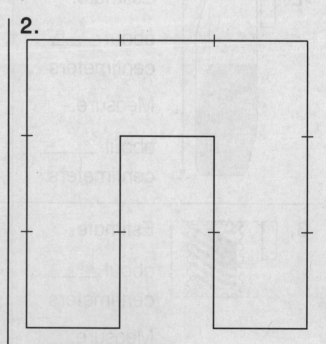

The perimeter
of the shape is _____ inches.

© Pearson Education, Inc. 1

How many triangle pattern blocks will cover this shape?
Check your answers to be sure they make sense.

Mai says 4 triangle
pattern blocks will
cover this shape.

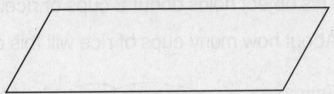

Does her answer make sense?

Check. Put triangle blocks
over the shape.

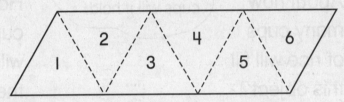

Circle the answer that makes sense.

  4 pattern blocks   (6 pattern blocks)

How many triangle pattern blocks will cover each shape?
Circle the answer that makes sense.

1.

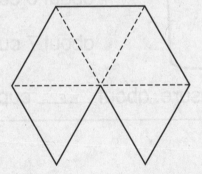

  (5 pattern blocks)

  8 pattern blocks

2.

  10 pattern blocks

  14 pattern blocks

© Pearson Education, Inc. 1

Name _____

Estimating, Measuring, and Comparing Capacity

This holds 1 cup of rice.

This object holds about 2 cups of rice.

About how many cups of rice will this object hold?

Estimate.

About how many cups of rice will fill this object?

Think: How many cups will it hold.

about __5__ cups

Measure.

How many cups of rice will fill the object?

Fill it with rice to measure.

about __6__ cups

Estimate how many cups of rice will fill each object.
Circle your estimate. Then measure.

1.

Estimate.

about 4 cups

(about 12 cups)

Measure. about _____ cups

2.

Estimate.

about 3 cups

about 7 cups

Measure. about _____ cups

Problem Solving *Estimation*

3. Circle the container that holds about 5 cups.

© Pearson Education, Inc. 1

Cups, Pints, and Quarts

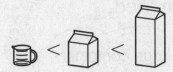 < <

Remember: < stands for less than.

Estimate. How much milk will fill the pitcher?

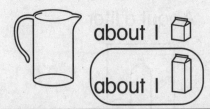

about 1

about 1

Circle the best estimate.

1.

about 1

about 1

2.

about 1

about 1

3.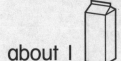

more than 1

less than 1

4.

more than 1

less than 1

© Pearson Education, Inc. 1

Liters

Estimate how much each real object will hold when filled.

A small container holds a little.

A large container holds a lot.

Less than a liter   About a liter   More than a liter

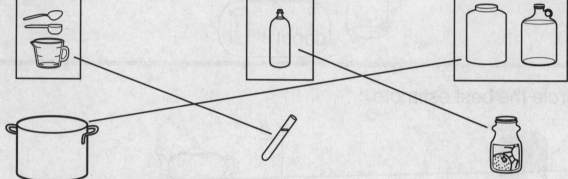

Draw a line to the best estimate.

1.

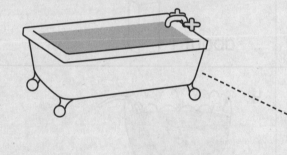

less than 1 liter

more than 1 liter

2.

less than 1 liter

more than 1 liter

3.

Apple Juice

less than 1 liter

more than 1 liter

© Pearson Education, Inc. 1

Name _____

Estimating, Measuring, and Comparing Weight

Does not balance.	Balances.	Does not balance.
	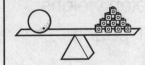	
The orange is heavier than 2 cubes.	9 cubes are as heavy as the orange.	20 cubes are heavier than the orange.

Estimate how many cubes it will take to balance.
Then measure.

1.

Estimate.

about _____ 🔲

Measure.

about _____ 🔲

2.

Estimate.

about _____ 🔲

Measure.

about _____ 🔲

3.

Estimate.

about _____ 🔲

Measure.

about _____ 🔲

4.

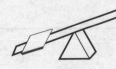

Estimate.

about _____ 🔲

Measure.

about _____ 🔲

© Pearson Education, Inc. 1

Pounds

This weight is 1 pound.

The light bulb weighs less than 1 pound.	The melon weighs about 1 pound.	The dog weighs more than 1 pound.

Circle the best estimate.

1.

less than 1 pound	more than 1 pound 

2.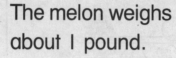

less than 1 pound	more than 1 pound

3.

less than 1 pound	more than 1 pound

© Pearson Education, Inc. 1

Grams and Kilograms

This feather measures about 1 gram.
1 gram is lighter than 1 kilogram.

This book measures about 1 kilogram.
1 kilogram is heavier than 1 gram.

Circle the best estimate.

1.

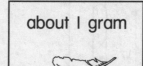
about 1 gram

about 1 kilogram

2.

about 1 gram
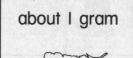

about 1 kilogram

3.

about 1 gram

about 1 kilogram

© Pearson Education, Inc. 1

Measuring Temperature

The colored part of a thermometer
measures the temperature.
It tells how hot or how cold it is.

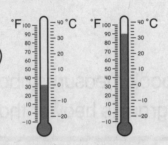

Not much of the colored
part means cold.

A lot of the colored
part means hot.

Circle the thermometer that shows the temperature.

1.

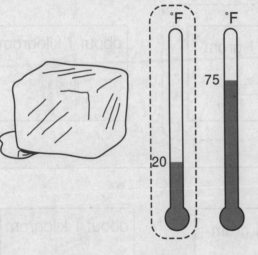

°F 75 20

°F

2.

°C 2

°C 34

3.

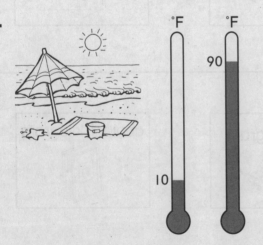

°F 90 10

°F

4.

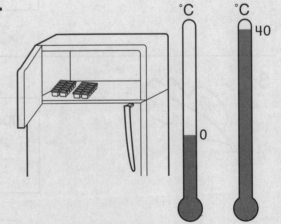

°C 0

°C 40

© Pearson Education, Inc. 1

Choosing a Measurement Tool

 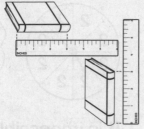 

| A thermometer measures how hot or cold it is. | A ruler measures how long or how tall an object is. | A scale measures how heavy an object is. | A measuring cup measures how much something can hold. |

Circle the best tool to use for the measurement.

1. How heavy is it?

  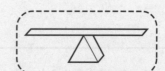

2. How long is it?

 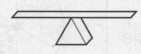 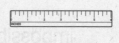

3. How hot is it?

 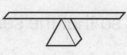

4. How much will it hold?

  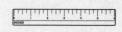

© Pearson Education, Inc. 1

Certain or Impossible

This spinner has only 3s on it.

I am certain to land on a 3.

This spinner has no 3s on it.

It is impossible for me to land on 3.

Are you certain to land on 4 or is it impossible?

1. 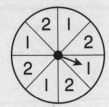 certain

(impossible)

2.  certain

impossible

Are you certain to land on black or is it impossible?

3.  certain

impossible

4. 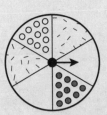 certain

impossible

Color the cubes so that the sentence is true.

5. It is impossible to pick a red cube.

© Pearson Education, Inc. 1

Name _____

More Likely or Less Likely

There are more gray cubes in the bag than there are white cubes.

Pick a cube.
Make a tally mark.
Put the cube back in the bag. Pick another cube.
Make a tally mark.
Put the cube back in the bag.

Color	Tally
Gray	II
White	

Since there are more gray cubes in the bag, it is more likely you will pick gray.

Fill a bag with 10 blue and 3 red cubes.
Pick a cube. Mark a tally for your pick.
Put the cube back. Do this 10 times.
Mark a tally for each pick.

1.

Color	Tally
Blue	
Red	

2. **Predict:** Which color cube is it more likely you will pick next?

_____

© Pearson Education, Inc. 1

Name _____

Stir-Fry It!

Japanese chopsticks are shorter than Chinese chopsticks. Japanese chopsticks are about 8 inches long. Is 8 inches more than 2 centimeters or less than 2 centimeters?

more than 2 centimeters

Check your answer.
Use your centimeter ruler to show
2 centimeters. Use your inch ruler
to show 8 inches.

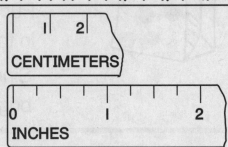

Does your answer make sense?

I don't need to show all 8 inches.
2 inches is longer than 2 centimeters.

yes

1. Jerry wants to make a pair of chopsticks.
   The chopsticks will be 8 inches long.
   The wood Jerry will use is 1 foot long.
   Is 8 inches more than a foot or less than a foot?

   _____

2. The wood cost 35¢. Jerry gave the clerk
   a quarter and 2 nickels. Did he get change? _____

Writing in Math

3. Ask the children in your class if they have ever eaten
   with chopsticks. Make a tally chart to show their answers.

© Pearson Education, Inc. 1

Doubles

When you add the same number to itself, you are using doubles.

◇
◇   1
  + 1
    2

◇ ◇
◇ ◇   2
   + 2
     4

◇ ◇ ◇
◇ ◇ ◇   3
    + 3
      6

◇ ◇ ◇ ◇
◇ ◇ ◇ ◇   4
     + 4
       8

Use doubles to add. Draw doubles to help you.

I. ◇ ◇ ◇ ◇ ◇
◇ ◇ ◇ ◇ ◇   5
      + 5
       10

2. ○ ○ ○ ○ ○ ○   6
       + 6

3. ○ ○ ○ ○ ○ ○ ○   7
        + 7

4. ○ ○ ○ ○ ○ ○ ○ ○   8
         + 8

Problem Solving *Visual Thinking*

5. For each picture write an addition sentence
that tells how many buttons there are.

__2__ + ____ = ____

____ + ____ = ____

© Pearson Education, Inc. 1

Doubles Plus 1 and Doubles Minus 1

You can use a doubles fact to help you add one more
or one less.

	Add 1 more to $4 + 4$.	Take 1 away from $4 + 4$.
4 $+ 4$ 8	4 $+ 5$ 9	4 $+ 3$ 7

Add 1 more or take 1 away from each doubles fact.

1.   3
  $+ 3$
  6

3
$+ 4$
7

3
$+ 2$
5

2.   5
  $+ 5$

5
$+ 6$

5
$+ 4$

3.   6
  $+ 6$

6
$+ 7$

6
$+ 5$

Problem Solving *Mental Math*

Answer each question.

4. Don has 8 red balloons.
He has 9 yellow balloons.
How many balloons does
Don have in all?

5. Kit has 5 blue balloons.
She has 4 orange balloons.
How many balloons does
Kit have in all?

_____ balloons

_____ balloons

© Pearson Education, Inc. 1

Adding 10

You can use tens to add.

This is one group of 10.	This is 10 and 1 more.	This is 10 and 3 more.
	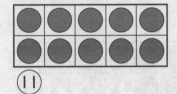	
10	$10 + 1 = 11$	$10 + 3 = 13$

Draw counters. Then find the sum.

1.

$10 + 5 = \underline{15}$

2.

$10 + 6 = \underline{}$

3.

$10 + 7 = \underline{}$

4.

$10 + 4 = \underline{}$

5.

$10 + 9 = \underline{}$

6.

$10 + 8 = \underline{}$

© Pearson Education, Inc. 1

Making 10 to Add

Making 10 can help you add.

Add 7 + 4.   Make a 10.

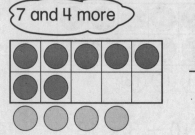   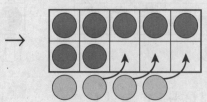   

So 7 + 4 and 10 + 1 have the same sum.

$$7 + 4 = \underline{11} \text{ and } 10 + 1 = \underline{11}$$

Use counters and Workmat 2.

Draw the counters. Then write the sums.

1.

$$\begin{array}{r} 8 \\ + 5 \\ \hline 13 \end{array}$$

$$\begin{array}{r} 10 \\ + 3 \\ \hline 13 \end{array}$$

2.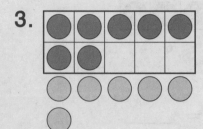

$$\begin{array}{r} 9 \\ + 6 \\ \hline \end{array}$$

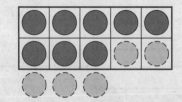

$$\begin{array}{r} 10 \\ + 5 \\ \hline \end{array}$$

3.

$$\begin{array}{r} 7 \\ + 6 \\ \hline \end{array}$$

$$\begin{array}{r} 10 \\ + 3 \\ \hline \end{array}$$

© Pearson Education, Inc. 1

Applying Addition Fact Strategies

6
+ 5

6 + 5 is close to 6 + 6. I can use doubles minus 1 to add.

6   ○○○○○○
+ 6   ○○○○○○
12

6   ○○○○○○
+ 5   ○○○○○⊗
11

9
+ 5

9 is close to 10. I can make a 10.

9
+ 5
14

9
+ 5
14

10
+ 4
14

Add. Then circle the strategy you used.

1.   8
   + 3
   11

doubles

(make a ten)

Think: 8 is close to 10.

2.   5
   + 4

doubles

make a ten

Think: 5 + 4 is close to 5 + 5. I can use doubles minus 1 to add.

3.   7
   + 5

doubles

make a ten

Think: 7 is close to 10. I can make a ten.

© Pearson Education, Inc. 1

Name _____

Adding Three Numbers

When you add three numbers, look for facts you know.
Then add the other number.

$\begin{array}{c}⑥\\④\end{array}$ $6 + 4 = 10$

$\begin{array}{c}\\+3\\\hline 13\end{array}$ $10 + 3 = 13$

(The numbers are in a different order.)

$\begin{array}{c}4\\③\end{array}$ $3 + 6 = 9$

$\begin{array}{c}+⑥\\\hline 13\end{array}$ $9 + 4 = 13$

(The sum is the same.)

Find each sum. Add the circled numbers first.
Then add the other number.

1. $\begin{array}{c}⑤\\2\\+⑤\\\hline 12\end{array}$ $5 + 5 = \underline{10}$

$\underline{10} + 2 = \underline{12}$

$\begin{array}{c}5\\②\\+⑤\\\hline 12\end{array}$ $2 + 5 = \underline{7}$

$\underline{7} + 5 = \underline{12}$

---

2. $\begin{array}{c}③\\⑥\\+4\end{array}$ $3 + 6 = \underline{\hspace{1cm}}$

$\underline{\hspace{1cm}} + 4 = \underline{\hspace{1cm}}$

$\begin{array}{c}3\\⑥\\+④\end{array}$ $6 + 4 = \underline{\hspace{1cm}}$

$\underline{\hspace{1cm}} + 3 = \underline{\hspace{1cm}}$

---

3. $\begin{array}{c}⑦\\③\\+4\end{array}$ $7 + 3 = \underline{\hspace{1cm}}$

$\underline{\hspace{1cm}} + 4 = \underline{\hspace{1cm}}$

$\begin{array}{c}7\\③\\+④\end{array}$ $3 + 4 = \underline{\hspace{1cm}}$

$\underline{\hspace{1cm}} + 7 = \underline{\hspace{1cm}}$

© Pearson Education, Inc. 1

PROBLEM-SOLVING STRATEGY
Make a Table

Jan is making groups of flowers. The flowers are red,
blue, and yellow. Each group has 3 flowers on it.
How many different groups can Jan make?

Read and Understand

You need to find how many different ways you can
put the flowers together.

Plan and Solve

You can make a table.

Count how many ways
you made.

There are _____ ways.

Red Flowers	Blue Flowers	Yellow Flowers
3	0	0
0	3	0
0	0	3
2	1	0
2	0	1

You can have 3 flowers of one color.

You can have 2 flowers of one color and 1 flower of another color.

You can have 1 flower of each color.

Look Back and Check

Did you find all the ways?
How can you check?

© Pearson Education, Inc. 1

Name _____

Using Related Facts

These two facts are related.

The addition sentence and the subtraction sentence have the same 3 numbers.

$9 + 3 = 12$

$12 - 3 = 9$

The sum of the addition sentence is the first number in the subtraction sentence.

Add. Then write a related subtraction fact.

1.

$8 + 4 = 12$

$12 - 4 = 8$

2.

$7 + 6 = 13$

$13 - 6 = $ ____

3.

$9 + 2 = $ ____

____ $- 9 = $ ____

4.

$8 + 5 = $ ____

____ $- 8 = $ ____

5.

$9 + 7 = $ ____

____ $- 9 = $ ____

6.

$8 + 7 = $ ____

____ $- 8 = $ ____

140 Use with Lesson 11-8.

© Pearson Education, Inc. 1

Fact Families

This is a fact family.

$8 + 4 = 12$

$4 + 8 = 12$

Each number sentence has the same 3 numbers.

$12 - 8 = 4$

$12 - 4 = 8$

Complete each fact family. Use counters to help you.

1. | 6 | 11 | 5 |

$6 + 5 = \underline{11}$

$5 + \underline{6} = 11$

$11 - 5 = \underline{6}$

$11 - \underline{6} = 5$

2. | 9 | 5 | 14 |

$9 + 5 = \underline{\hspace{1cm}}$

$5 + \underline{\hspace{1cm}} = 14$

$14 - 5 = \underline{\hspace{1cm}}$

$14 - \underline{\hspace{1cm}} = 5$

3. | 7 | 6 | 13 |

$7 + 6 = \underline{\hspace{1cm}}$

$6 + \underline{\hspace{1cm}} = 13$

$13 - 6 = \underline{\hspace{1cm}}$

$13 - \underline{\hspace{1cm}} = 6$

© Pearson Education, Inc. 1

Name _____

Using Addition to Subtract

$6 + 5 = 11$ $11 - 5 = \underline{6}$

You can use an addition fact to help you write
a subtraction fact with the same numbers.

Add. Then use the addition fact to help you subtract.
Use cubes if you like.

1. $4 + 9 = \underline{13}$

   $13 - 9 = \underline{4}$

2. $8 + 7 = \underline{}$

   $15 - 7 = \underline{}$

3. $7 + 4 = \underline{}$

   $11 - 4 = \underline{}$

4. $6 + 7 = \underline{}$

   $13 - 7 = \underline{}$

© Pearson Education, Inc. 1

Using 10 to Subtract

Subtract 13 − 7.

Cross out 7.　　　　　　　　　What is left?

13
−7

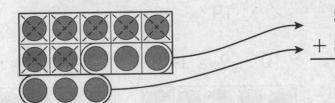

　　3
+ 3
　　6

13
−7
──
　6

─────────────────────────────

Cross out to subtract. Use counters if you like.

1. 11
　　− 8

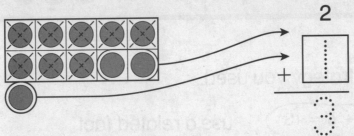

　　2
+ ⋮
──
　3

11
− 8
──

2. 17
　　− 9

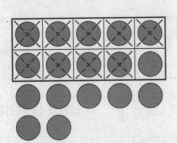

　　1
+ ☐
──
☐

17
− 9
──

3. 15
　　− 7

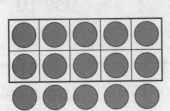

☐
☐
+ ☐
──

15
− 7
──

4. 16
　　− 8

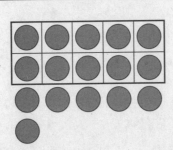

☐
☐
+ ☐
──

16
− 8
──

© Pearson Education, Inc. 1

Name _____

Applying Subtraction Fact Strategies

R 11-12

14
− 9
_____

> I know that 9 + 5 = 14.
> I can use the related
> fact to find 14 − 9.

9   ○○○○○○○○
+ 5 ●●●●●
____
14

14   ⊠⊠⊠⊠⊠⊠⊠⊠⊠○○○○○
− 9
____
5

$$10 - 9 = 1$$

$$1 + 4 = 5$$

14
− 9
_____

> I can use 10
> to subtract.

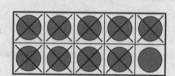

14
− 9
____
5

Subtract.

Then circle the strategy you used.

1.   13
    − 7
    _____
    6

> 7 + 6 = 13

use a related fact

> 10 − 7 = 3
> 3 + 3 = 6

use 10

---

2.   14
    − 6

use a related fact

use 10

3.   12
    − 5

use a related fact

use 10

---

4.   15
    − 6

use a related fact

use 10

5.   17
    − 9

use a related fact

use 10

© Pearson Education, Inc. 1

144   Use with Lesson 11-12.

Name _____

Multiple-Step Problems

Jill has 6 marbles. She gets 5 more.
How many marbles does she have in all?

$6 + 5 = \underline{11}$ marbles

Jill gives 8 marbles to Sal.
Now how many marbles
does Jill have?

Think: I know Jill has 11 marbles in all. I know she gives 8 to Sal. I can subtract to find how many she has left.

$11 - 8 = \underline{3}$ Jill has $\underline{3}$ marbles left.

Solve each problem.

1. Jack has 4 model cars. He gets 3 more model cars.
   How many model cars does Jack have in all?

   $\underline{3} + \underline{4} = \underline{7}$ model cars

   For his birthday Jack gets 5 model cars.
   How many model cars does he have now?

   _____ + _____ = _____ model cars

---

2. Nicky has 6 charms on her bracelet. She buys 8 more.
   How many charms does Nicky have in all?

   _____ + _____ = _____ charms

   On the way home 4 charms are lost.
   How many charms does Nicky have now?

   _____ − _____ = _____ charms

© Pearson Education, Inc. 1

Name _____

On the Farm

There are 12 hens in a barnyard.
4 hens are brown. The rest are white.
How many hens are white?

$12 - 4 =$ __8__

Use a related addition fact to check your answer.

$4 + 8 =$ __12__   So, $12 - 4 =$ __8__.

---

1. 4 cows are in the barn.   4
   7 cows are in the pen.   7
   3 cows are in the meadow. $+\ 3$
   How many cows are there in all?   _____ cows

---

2. The farmer has 17 baskets   Check
   of strawberries.   17
   He sells 9 baskets. $-\ 9$ $+$
   How many baskets are left?   17   _____ baskets

Writing in Math

3. Draw a picture of 14 eggs. Write a
   subtraction story about your picture.
   Then write a number sentence.

   _____

   _____

   _____ − _____ = _____

© Pearson Education, Inc. 1

Adding Groups of 10

You can use what you know about adding ones
to add groups of ten.

2 ones and 5 ones are 7 ones.   2 tens and 5 tens are 7 tens.

$$2 \ + \ 5 \ = \ 7 \qquad 20 \ + \ 50 \ = \ 70$$

Write each number sentence.

1.

$$\underline{3} \ + \ \underline{2} \ = \ \underline{5} \qquad \underline{30} \ + \ \underline{20} \ = \ \underline{50}$$

2.

$$\underline{} \ + \ \underline{} \ = \ \underline{6} \qquad \underline{} \ + \ \underline{} \ = \ \underline{60}$$

3.

$$\underline{} \ + \ \underline{} \ = \ \underline{} \qquad \underline{} \ + \ \underline{} \ = \ \underline{}$$

4.

$$\underline{} \ + \ \underline{} \ = \ \underline{}$$

5.

$$\underline{} \ + \ \underline{} \ = \ \underline{}$$

© Pearson Education, Inc. 1

Adding Tens to Two-Digit Numbers

You can count on by tens to add.

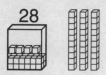

3 tens

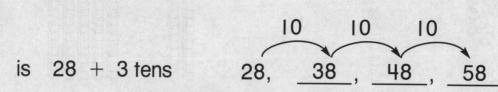

28 + 30   is   28 + 3 tens   28, __38__ , __48__ , __58__

28 + 30 = 58

Solve each number sentence.

1.

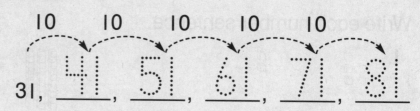

31, __41__ , __51__ , __61__ , __71__ , __81__

31 + 50   is   31 + __5__ tens

31 + 50 = __81__

2. 52

52 + 20   is 52 + ____ tens   52, ____ , ____

52 + 20 = ____

3.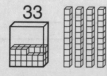

33 + 40 is 33 + ____ tens   33, ____ , ____ , ____ , ____

33 + 40 = ____

© Pearson Education, Inc. 1

Adding Two-Digit Numbers

Find the sum of 25 and 13.

	Add the ones.	Add the tens.

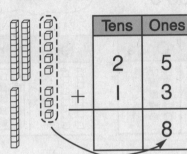

Tens	Ones
2	5
+ 1	3

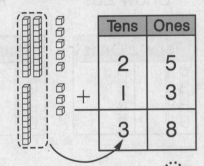

Tens	Ones
2	5
+ 1	3
	8

Tens	Ones
2	5
+ 1	3
3	8

$5 + 3 = \underline{8}$

$2 + 1 = \underline{3}$

$25 + 13 = \underline{38}$

$20 + 10 = \underline{30}$

Draw and add the ones and tens. Find each sum.

1. Find the sum of 43 and 24.

Add the ones.		Add the tens.

Tens	Ones
+	

Tens	Ones
+	

Tens	Ones
+	

_____ + _____ = _____

_____ + _____ = _____

$43 + 24 = \underline{\qquad}$

_____ + _____ = _____

© Pearson Education, Inc. 1

Regrouping in Addition

Add 26 and 5.

Show 26.   Add 5.

Regroup 10 ones as 1 ten.

Tens	Ones

Tens	Ones

Tens	Ones

Tens	Ones

$26 + 5 = \underline{31}$

Find the sum.

1. Add 16 and 7.

Show 16.   Add 7.   Regroup.   Find the sum.

Tens	Ones

Tens	Ones

Tens	Ones

Tens	Ones

$16 + 7 = \underline{23}$

---

2. Add 28 and 5.

Show 28.   Add 5.   Regroup.   Find the sum.

Tens	Ones

Tens	Ones

Tens	Ones

Tens	Ones

$28 + 5 = \underline{\hspace{2cm}}$

© Pearson Education, Inc. 1

PROBLEM-SOLVING SKILL

Exact Answer or Estimate?

Al has 2 bags of name tags.

Each bag has 12 name tags.

There are 18 children in his group.

Does he have enough name tags for all of the children?

Read and Understand

You need to know if 2 bags of name tags
are enough for 18 children.

Do you need an exact answer or an estimate?

Plan and Solve

12 is more than 10, so 12 + 12 is greater than 10 + 10.

18 is less than 10 + 10. You can estimate that there are enough.

exact answer   (estimate)

Look Back and Check

Does your answer make sense?

Is an exact answer or an estimate needed
to solve each problem?

Circle **exact answer** or **estimate.**

1. Jody wants to buy 4 stickers.
   They cost 7¢ each. Jody
   has 45¢. Does she have
   enough money?

   exact answer   estimate

2. Jody has 12 stickers.
   She has 3 pages left in her
   sticker book. Can she put
   4 stickers on each page?

   exact answer   estimate

© Pearson Education, Inc. 1

Subtracting Groups of 10

Subtracting groups of 10 is like subtracting ones.

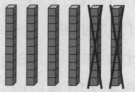

6 − 2 = __4__

60 − 20 = __40__

Complete each number sentence.

1.

5 − 1 = __4__   50 − 10 = __40__

2.

6 − 3 = _____   60 − 30 = _____

3.

7 − 4 = _____   70 − 40 = _____

4.

5 − 4 = _____   50 − 40 = _____

Problem Solving *Mental Math*

Solve.

5. A star sticker and a sun sticker cost 50¢ altogether.
The star sticker costs 20¢ by itself. How much does
the sun sticker cost?

_____¢

© Pearson Education, Inc. 1

Subtracting Tens from Two-Digit Numbers

You can count back by tens to subtract.

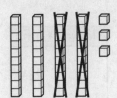

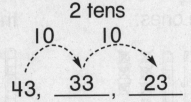

2 tens

10   10

43, _33_ , _23_

43 − 20   is   43 − 2 tens

43 − 20 = _23_

Solve each number sentence.

1.

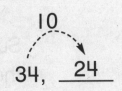

10

34, _24_

34 − 10   is   34 − __|__ ten

34 − 10 = _24_

2.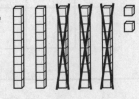

10

52, ____, ____, ____

52 − 30   is   52 − ____ tens

52 − 30 = ____

3.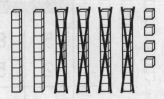

64, ____, ____, ____, ____

64 − 40   is   64 − ____ tens

64 − 40 = ____

© Pearson Education, Inc. 1

Subtracting Two-Digit Numbers

Find the difference for 38 − 16.

Tens	Ones
3	8
− 1	6
	2

Subtract the ones.

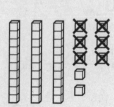

Subtract the tens.

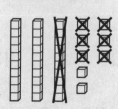

Tens	Ones
3	8
− 1	6
2	2

Write each difference.

1.

Tens	Ones
4	6
− 3	2

Subtract the ones.

Subtract the tens.

Tens	Ones
4	6
− 3	2

2.

Tens	Ones
5	8
− 2	5

Subtract the ones.

Subtract the tens.

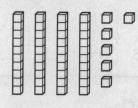

Tens	Ones
5	8
− 2	5

© Pearson Education, Inc. 1

Regrouping In Subtraction

Find the difference for the problem 32 − 6.

Show 32.

Tens	Ones

Subtract 6.

Regroup 1 ten as 10 ones.

Tens	Ones

Subtract.

Tens	Ones

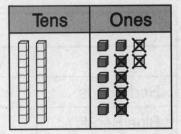

$32 - 6 = \underline{26}$

I. Find the difference for the problem 46 − 8.

Show 46.

Tens	Ones

Subtract 8.

Regroup.

Tens	Ones

Subtract.

Tens	Ones

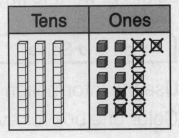

$46 - 8 = \underline{38}$

---

2. Find the difference for the problem 23 − 7.

Show 23.

Tens	Ones

Subtract 7.

Regroup.

Tens	Ones

Subtract.

Tens	Ones

$23 - 7 = \underline{\qquad}$

© Pearson Education, Inc. 1

PROBLEM-SOLVING STRATEGY

Make a Graph

The bead store sells red, white, and blue beads. Which color bead did they sell the most?

> Count by tens. Then count on by fives.

Beads Sold				
	Week 1	Week 2	Week 3	Week 4
Red Beads	10	5	10	10
Blue Beads	10	5	5	10
White Beads	10	10	10	10

Read and Understand

The chart shows how many of each color beads were sold. We want to find which color sold the most.

Plan and Solve

Use the information in the chart to make a graph.
Color one box for every 5 beads sold.

> Count the boxes by fives.

Beads Sold

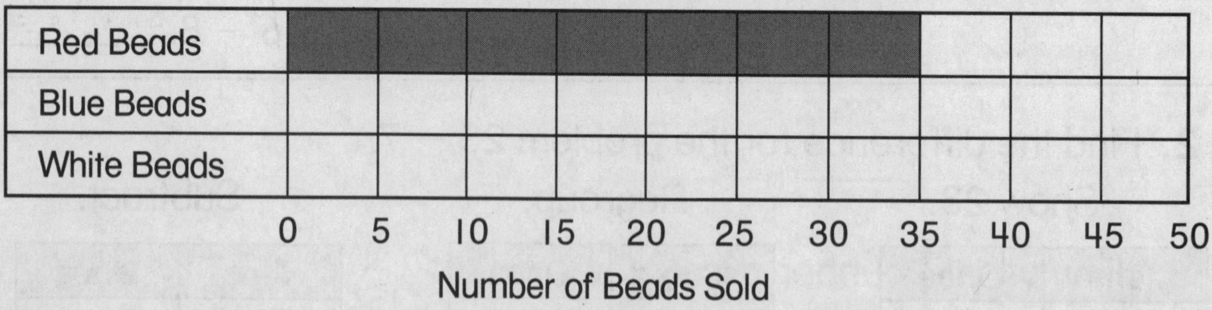

Red Beads										
Blue Beads										
White Beads										

0   5   10   15   20   25   30   35   40   45   50
Number of Beads Sold

The _____ beads sold the most.

Look Back and Check

How can you be sure your answer is correct?

© Pearson Education, Inc. 1

PROBLEM-SOLVING APPLICATIONS

Caring for Kittens

The Kitty-Cat Pet Shop has 23 squeaky cat toys.
The store owner buys 20 more squeaky cat toys.
How many squeaky cat toys does the pet shop
have altogether?

23 and __20__ more is how many altogether?

Use counting on by ten to add: 23 $+$ __20__ $=$ __43__

The pet shop has __43__ squeaky cat toys.

---

1. On Monday, the Kitty-Cat Pet Shop
   sold 10 squeaky cat toys. How many
   squeaky cat toys does the store have left?

   ____ ◯ ____ = ____ squeaky cat toys

2. Jimmy bought 5 white rubber mice
   and 4 blue rubber mice. How many
   rubber mice did he buy?

   ____ ◯ ____ = ____ rubber mice

3. Jimmy lost 2 rubber mice. How many
   rubber mice does he have left?

   ____ ◯ ____ = ____ rubber mice

© Pearson Education, Inc. 1